LAP QUILTING
with Georgia Bonesteel

LAP QUILTING
with Georgia Bonesteel

Oxmoor House, Inc.
Birmingham

To my family:
*May they discover the gratification and joy in what-
ever they pursue that I have found in quilting.*

To my sister, mother and father and friends:
Thank you for your help, guidance and tolerance.

To my students:
May they "gallop and grin" forever.

Copyright© 1982 Oxmoor House, Inc.
Book Division of Southern Progress Corporation
P.O. Box 2463, Birmingham, Alabama 35201

Library of Congress Catalog Number: 81-83054
ISBN: 0-8487-0524-6
Manufactured in the United States of America
Sixth Printing 1984

ISBN 0-8487-0524-6

Contents

The 25-Patch Star design in an optional diagonal setting with a pieced outside border.

Introduction

Quilting. Does the word conjure up cozy church parlors with friends gathered around a quilting frame? . . . hours of timeless handwork for a pieced top that still needs to be quilted? . . . a barn in Pennsylvania Dutch country filled with Amish women in bonnets silently sewing?

Well, not anymore! Now, you'll find us quilting in airplanes, doctors' offices, laundromats, the car—anywhere today's quilter can steal some precious time. We are doing Lap Quilting, the portable quilting concept so compatible with today's life-style.

Lap quilting is the technique of joining three layers—a decorative top, batting, and backing—together in small, block-sized sections that are then connected to form the entire quilt.

For a group, the quilting bee serves an obvious purpose. But many quilters want a more personal project, something of their own, and a large quilt seems an awesome feat. Few of us have room for a big quilting frame, and so many

of us work outside the home, leaving us with limited craft time. Working in smaller sections, quilting as you go, has obvious appeal.

I learned to sew at my mother's knee; I learned to quilt through serendipity! I was making neckties for my husband and had many triangular leftovers perfect for patchwork pillows. One day a friend gave me another box full of necktie remnants and challenged me to "create something." After a number of trips to the drawing board and a lot of flimsy piecework, I discovered that layering material with batting and backing creates body. Hand stitching and quilting produces depth and dimension. Hooray! This was Lap Quilting.

The first results were several quilted evening bags very much like those pictured here. The

Opposite: *Blue sampler quilt with inside mitered borders and contrasting bias edging.*
Left: *The author quilting a lap-sized quilt block with her cat, Chi-Chi.*
Above: *Crazy patch evening bags were the author's first attempts at lap quilting.*

Lavender Lullaby is a sampler quilt with inside mitered borders.

richness of the tie silk colors gave a jewellike quality to the bags. Once, while traveling, I noticed a gentleman double-check his necktie. No wonder. I was placing a fin 'n feather stitch on the very same fabric for a handbag!

A move to North Carolina found me teaching sewing at a technical college. I was still quilting small handbags in my spare time for several boutiques and getting the urge to try bigger projects.

The next step seemed natural—I decided to offer a quilting class. I sat in at quilting bees, checked quilting books out from the library, reviewed history and terminology, ordered my standing frame, and awaited my first students. I soon realized there was no way each student could finish a quilt on a frame in an eleven-week class that met only once a week for three hours. After many trials and errors, I refined my

method of lap quilting. We could build an entire quilt by adding sections gradually, each student working at her own pace.

My goal is to teach you this technique and share the classroom experiences of ten years. I remain devoted to and continually inspired by my students. Their comments continually remind me that quilts do more than warm our bones on chilly evenings; they warm our hearts with remembrances of times long gone.

Your own level of perfection in any handwork comes from experience. For instance, the more you quilt, the smaller your stitches. Experiment with templates, try new patterns and unusual color combinations, attend a seminar, collect books, take courses from more than one teacher—all will help you create your own unique style.

Now, let's make a quilt!

Starting from Scratch

There is orderliness and direction in patchwork, and they hold a special appeal for me. The faucet can drip, the creek can rise, and the sewing room can be a mess—but I have control over the outcome of my pieced blocks. Selecting the design, choosing the fabric, cutting the pieces, and watching the quilt develop are some of the steps toward the finished product.

Being proud and secure in your work starts with an understanding of quilt definitions. Let's take a look at some basic quilting and sewing terminology.

TERMS

Appliqué—Cutout figures sewn to a larger foundation piece of material. The application can be made in several ways: basting under raw edges and then securing with a hidden slip stitch; buttonhole stitching on top of raw edges; working raw edges under ⅛", clipping curves and attaching with a slip stitch. Machine embroidery with a zig-zag may also be used. Page 27 introduces a new variation—partly pieced and partly appliquéd—to the classic Little Dutch Girl and Little Dutch Boy.

Backing—The bottom or back layer of a quilt; the underneath side. Muslin is a popular fabric for the backing because it highlights the quilting stitches and large quantities of muslin can be purchased inexpensively. Dark colored backings are risky for a beginner using white thread, as the stitch length becomes predominant. Print fabrics tend to hide the stitches completely. In lap quilting, a design can be created on the back of the quilt by alternating stripes or the pattern of the blocks. Be careful of certain fabrics such as large checks or prints where the horizontal and the vertical of the pattern will deviate and not run true.

Backstitch—Used in hand piecing to strengthen a running stitch; done with a single thread by simply inserting the point of the nee-

dle behind the thread each time and coming up ahead. Also used in ending off quilting. When out of thread, loop the thread and form a knot close to the fabric; then backstitch into the quilt top and pull a floater thread through the batting, coming back up about an inch away; clip off. (Figure 1.)

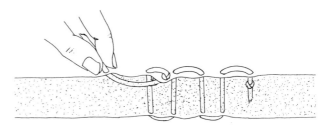

Figure 1

Baste—A temporary running stitch used to secure fabric prior to machine stitching or hand quilting. It is best done with a contrasting thread that will be easy to see when removing. Some black cotton threads will leave a tiny black spot upon removal, so test your basting thread. A very important feature of lap quilting, basting sets the stage for quilting, with or without a frame or hoop.

Batting—The filler or middle part of the quilt sandwich—the insulation. Today, polyester batting is most widely used and is available in various weights and thicknesses. No matter what type you prefer to use, make sure that your batting has been bonded.

Block—A unit of patchwork, usually in the form of a square, repeated to construct the entire quilt top. Blocks may be attached to each other (block-to-block assembly) or may be separated by borders.

Block-to-Block Assembly—In lap quilting, the process of joining already quilted blocks to form horizontal or vertical rows.

Borders—Narrow panels that set off each block in a quilt. The corners of borders may be mitered or squared off with small squares in a contrasting color. Borders may have appliqué accents or can be pieced to create a new design. Borders may also be added to the perimeter of a quilt that needs more length or width. (See page 65.)

Cross Hatch—Diagonal and right angled straight lines created on the quilt top as a guide for hand quilting.

Crazy Patch—A form of patchwork in which odd shapes of fabric are attached to a foundation block on the sewing machine. Embroidery stitches are then applied to accent the seam lines. String quilts also fall into this category. (See page 53.)

Dangling Thread—A loose, unknotted thread left in a quilted area to be rethreaded once the quilt is assembled in order to complete quilting and end off.

"Dog Ears"—The triangular extensions formed at the points where diagonal pieces are sewn together. Clipping them relieves the block of extra bulk.

Edging—Strips of fabric such as bias tape used to enclose the perimeter of a quilt. (See page 90.)

Grainline—The direction of the weave or construction of the yarns in fabric. Warp yarns form the lengthwise pull of the fabric and run parallel to the selvage, while the weft yarns form the right angle, interlacing to construct the material. Any line on the fabric that is not parallel to either the warp or weft yarns is considered to be off grain.

Marking—The process of transferring designs onto the quilt top in order to have a line to follow when quilting. Marking implements include fabric marker, water soluble pen (test your fabric first), thin slivers of soap, pencils, Contact® paper cut in special shapes, and masking tape. (See page 67.) The goal is for the hand quilting to dominate and the marking line to disappear.

Mitering—Creating a diagonal seam at the corner of a border to form a right angle. (See page 65.)

Off Hand—The hand that rests under the quilt, guiding the needle and feeling that all three layers have been caught by it. The finger that feels the point of the needle repeatedly should be protected with a thimble, masking tape, a coat of clear nail polish, or the fingertip from an old leather glove.

Patchwork—The art of building a large piece of decorative cloth from smaller pieces.

Piecing or Piecework—The process of sewing two or more pieces of fabric together. Done on the sewing machine with a regular length stitch, coordinating thread, and a ¼" seam allowance. Masking tape placed ¼" from the eye of the needle on the machine throat plate helps maintain even seam allowances. (See page 55.)

Quilt—Any bedcover with three layers; a sandwich comprised of the decorative top, the filler or batting, and the bottom layer or backing. These layers are secured with running stitches (quilting) or with yarn knots (tufting).

Row-to-Row Assembly—In lap quilting, the process of setting together rows of blocks (see Block-to-Block Assembly) to form a quilt. (See page 89.)

Setting—The relationship of one block to the next; the arrangement of blocks that forms the quilt top.

Stencil—Designs on paper that are transferred to the top, decorative part of a quilt providing a guide for quilting stitches. See page 67 for complete methods of stencil transfer to the fabric. For specific designs, see page 68.

Template—A pattern made from durable material (cardboard, plastic, sandpaper, or soft vinyl) used to transfer patchwork shapes onto fabric. Templates are a key factor in precision piecework, ensuring uniformity in size and shape. See page 54 for instructions on making templates. For patterns, see page 30.

Trapunto—A softly sculptured effect created by stuffing a design from the back or underside, giving the pattern more dimension.

NECESSITIES

Check your sewing basket; you'll already have many of the following items on hand. Two "necessities" not available at the notions counter are a strong desire to make a quilt and the patience to stick with it when piecework goes askew.

Batting: Polyester batting or filler comes in rolled sheets that are unfolded and cut in sections in preparation for quilting. It can be pieced in the middle as the odd shapes will be secured by your quilting stitches.

Embroidery floss: For appliqué and crazy patchwork. Use three of the six strands.

Hoops: Used to hold fabric for quilting. Optional in lap quilting, depending on your expertise in handling the basted, layered material. They come in round, oval, and square frames.

Iron: Steam iron and ironing board.

Masking tape: All widths can be used on fabric as a guide for quilting; ¼″-wide tape is especially helpful on the machine throat plate to maintain an even seam allowance.

Needles: "Quilting Betweens," sizes 7, 8, 9, 10 and even 11, with large eyes. Embroidery needles and sewing needles for basting.

Pencils, fabric marker, tailor's chalk, slivers of worn soap: Used to mark quilting designs on the fabric. Be sure to test all fabrics with the marking implement you intend to use to be sure it can be easily removed.

Pins: Large, white, round-head pins work well as they slip through fabric easily and are easy to find on deep carpet.

Ruler: A clear plastic ruler with a ¼″ marking on the straight edge; available at stationery stores.

Scissors: Good fabric scissors (hide from the family) and paper scissors for cutting out templates.

Thimbles: One for the middle finger of the hand that guides the needle, plus another to protect the underneath finger on the off hand.

Thread for quilting: Cotton or the polyester-wrapped quilting thread with a wax coating. Additional beeswax may be applied as each thread length is cut.

Thread for sewing machine: Dual duty, all-purpose thread. Do not use quilting thread on the sewing machine. Neutral colors such as gray, beige, and taupe blend with many fabric colors.

MAKING A CATHEDRAL CHATELAINE

Lap quilting is portable, and so should be your scissors, thread, needles and thimble. What better way to transport them than a pocket attached to a grosgrain ribbon worn around the neck? This scissors forget-me-not can be worn not just for quilting, but for any other needle fun, and also makes a great gift or bazaar item. It's a lap quilting trademark made with the cathedral quilt concept. Here's how.

Chatelaines made with the cathedral quilting concept. A chatelaine is a clasp or hook for keys, a watch, or in this case, a lap quilter's scissors and pins.

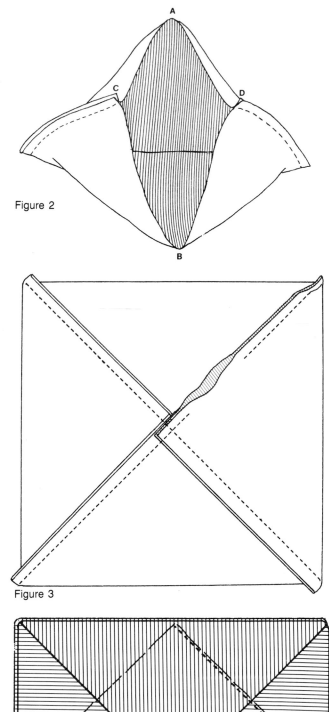

Figure 2

MATERIALS:
1 yard of grosgrain ribbon
Two 10″ squares of dark calico
Two 4½″ squares of contrasting fabric
Small amount of Velcro®

METHOD:
Turn raw edge of one end of the ribbon under ¼″ and sew Velcro® on top, using matching thread; 1″ further up the ribbon, sew another piece of Velcro®; attach scissors in the loop created.

Prepare Cathedral Pocket. For each 10″ square: Fold square into a rectangle, right sides together. Sew ¼″ seam allowance at each end. (Figure 1.)

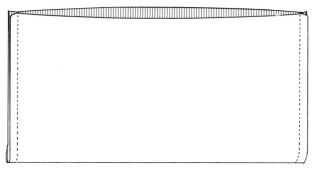

Figure 1

Figure 3

Pull the rectangle open at points A and B; bring C and D together; pin at intersection, letting piece fall into a triangle. (Figure 2.) Sew across the top, leaving a 2″ opening at the center. (Figure 3.) Turn right side out, press, stagger seams at the center, and slip stitch opening closed.

Find midpoint of each side. Connect these points, drawing a square within the square with a pencil or other marking device.

Center a Velcro® strip just inside one of the newly marked lines on the seamless side of one square. Do the same on the second square, but this time catch the free end of the grosgrain ribbon under the strip. Machine stitch each strip into place.

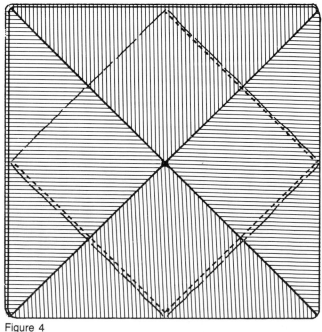

Figure 4

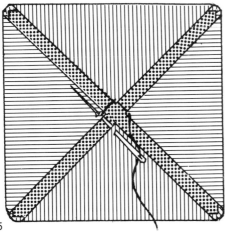
Figure 5

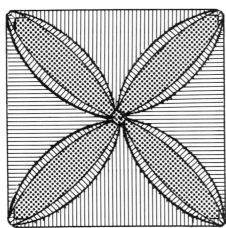
Figure 6

Align the two squares, seamless sides together. Machine stitch together in U shape formed by three marked lines, leaving open the line on which the Velcro® was attached. (Figure 4.)

Place a 4½″ square of contrasting fabric on each side of the square, lining up at the marked lines.

On each side, fold the four bordering triangles down over the new patch. Connect their tips. (Figure 5.)

Turn each bias edge back, revealing the inside color. Taking care not to go through to the pocket inside, slip stitch the curves in place. (A piece of cardboard placed in the pocket will help you avoid stitching through the pocket.) Whip stitch at the outside corner of each curve to conceal raw edges. (Figure 6.)

Card Tricks design with optional square insets on inside borders and saw-toothed edging.

FABRICS

Which comes first, the chicken or the egg? Do you first choose the pattern for a quilt and then the fabric, or just the opposite? It is a very fortunate quilter who begins a quilt with that decision already made.

Quite often I am asked, "Will you choose my colors for a quilt? What design is best for a first quilt? What is the secret of fabric selection?" Such personal decisions are hard to counsel. If you are in a similar quandary, expose yourself to quilts through the library, museums, friends,

Three sampler quilts with inside mitered borders.

Many Miters, a freehand adaptation of the Log Cabin design using a series of mitered borders.

magazines, and books. Make notes on your favorite colors and patterns and those that leave you cold. Then decide.

The pioneer woman had to select from whatever was on hand—a worn-out blanket, scraps from overalls, precious leftovers from a frock. Today we have a wealth of fabrics available along with a rich legacy of quilt patterns. This abundance, it's true, can make the decision overwhelming—however, there are some guidelines and suggestions that will help.

First, look at what you have on hand. All of us who sew have piles of remnants we squirrel away until the day we can find something to do with them.

When making your fabric selection, eliminate very sheer fabrics and heavy fabrics such as velvet, corduroy, and polyester. Save knit fabrics for another project where raw edges can be overlapped and either hand stitched or machine zigzagged in place; their bulk, thickness, and stretch qualities will not adapt to small piecework where more than two layers connect.

All-cotton fabrics or cotton blends are wonderful for machine piecework and hand quilting. Good quality fabric, especially in muslin, is very important.

Before you get started, preshrink your leftover scraps. Machine wash them in warm water, using the normal cycle and a small amount of soap. Then partially dry and steam press them. There will be strings, of course. You can use this same procedure for newly purchased fabric; it ensures a washable quilt and also softens the fabric for the needle. Eliminate any fabric (keep an eye on reds and blacks) that fades or bleeds.

Separate your preshrunk fabrics into color groups and sort them into plastic bags or small laundry bins. You may find that you have enough of a favorite calico to make it the springboard for a quilt design.

QUILT DESIGN

A sampler quilt can be the perfect choice for your first quilt. Each block represents a different story encased in a separate, mitered border with its own color scheme. Your inaugural quilt will be a true sampling of bygone blocks—a genuine tribute to traditional quilting. By using leftovers, your quilt becomes a memory quilt composed of sentimental, favorite fabrics. A colorful sampler has another feature—it will fit into any color scheme with a folksy, old-time look.

Keep in mind a balance of colors. Even though your sampler will be a hodgepodge of fabric, one color could dominate and become the central theme.

You may, on the other hand, want to achieve a specific color scheme in a quilt with the sampler concept. In this case, choose four coordinated fabrics—a print and a geometric design such as a small check, stripe, or polka dot; and two solid colors to blend with them. Choose twenty of your favorite blocks and go to it. You'll have the experience of learning how a number of different blocks are set together, but the result will be one color story. I call this a "sampler theme quilt."

You may decide on ten different blocks alternated with either one specific block or a stenciled design on a solid 12½″ square. Or a medallion effect can be achieved by highlighting four blocks in the center, bordering them with contrasting blocks. You are limited only by your imagination. But whatever design you choose, be sure to diagram on paper the blocks you plan to use and how you wish to set them together.

Borders can also change the outcome of a quilt. Consider a small check border (do not choose a large check since check material is woven with a distinct difference in crosswise and lengthwise grain), a print border, an eyelet border or alternating colors on each border.

Another point to consider in your color selection is your overall decor and home decorating scheme. What is your life-style and how will your quilt adapt to that style? Do you have pets, toddlers, or teenagers? Is your quilt going to be draped over a velvet love seat as a show-and-tell example of your handiwork, or will it be used every day for warmth?

Is there a favorite color you just cannot live without? One of my students has a passion for lavender; we have even accused her of dreaming in purple. And, of course, she has many lavender quilted items. Recently at a local quilting demonstration, a couple was in doubt about color and I couldn't help but observe their dress. The gentleman had on beige check pants, a cream shirt and a tan sweater; his wife was dressed all in beige and taupe. The answer was obvious—a monochromatic off-white color scheme would be the best for them.

Perhaps your wallpaper can guide you in making your color selection coordinate with an already decorated area. Keep in mind your bedroom walls. If they are bright white, perhaps muslin borders and backing would not be appropriate. Don't forget your carpeting or other room colors.

Some beginners prefer print fabrics that camouflage the quilting, but the design of the quilting is often hidden on them and not appreciated. My personal color favorites are muslin, white, or pastel, since the hand stitching is truly highlighted.

After making a sampler you will, no doubt, find a favorite pattern. This is your chance to make an entire shoo-fly or log cabin quilt using scraps or fabric purchased to compliment your color scheme.

Patchwork Designs & Patterns

BLOCK REQUIREMENTS

All of the quilts demonstrated in this book are based on a 12″ square. Through trial and error, I have found this to be a good size not only for quilts, but also for accessories. Keep in mind that not all of the blocks in this chapter are offered with the beginner in mind. Those blocks with more pattern pieces and curves will take more time and expertise, from cutting and sewing to quilting.

Blocks can be used two ways in lap quilting: Method A, with 3½″ borders on all four sides, producing an 18½″ square (Figure 1); or Method B, four 12″ blocks sewn together forming a 24″ square (Figure 2). Any size larger than

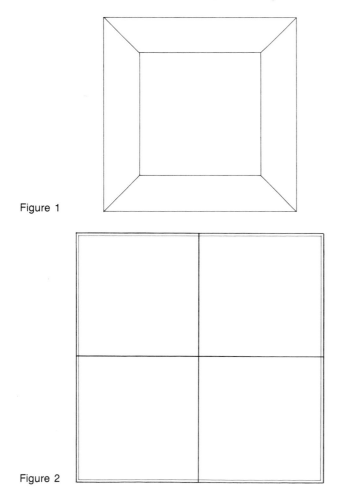

Figure 1

Figure 2

24″ becomes too awkward to quilt in your lap, even if you choose to work with a frame.

The sizes listed below apply to a quilt that will keep you warm in bed. If you want your quilt to cover both the mattress and the box spring, or if your bed is an odd size, measure your bed accurately. Divide both the width and the length of your bed by your chosen block size, either 18″ or 24″, and multiply these numbers to come up with the necessary number of blocks. These measurements do not allow for take-up in quilting—about ½″ per block.

Much depends on how you intend to use the quilt—as a total bed cover or folded to accent the end of the bed. If, after measuring the bed, you wish to alter the size of the finished quilt, change the width of the borders around each block, making wider and longer borders for a larger quilt or smaller borders to reduce the quilt size. If your border is increased by 1″ around each block, 6″ will be added to the width of a single bed quilt and 10″ to its length. That quilt would then measure 60″ x 100″. Borders should be 4½″ x 21″ in this case. After layering and lap quilting, each block will be 20″.

Plan ahead and measure carefully to give yourself a master plan; it is disappointing to end up with the wrong size quilt.

METHOD A

The following measurements apply to the 18″ square blocks (3″ borders attached to a 12″ block).

Baby quilt	36″ x 54″	6 blocks	2 across x 3 down
Afghan size	54″ x 72″	12 blocks	3 across x 4 down
Twin size	54″ x 90″	15 blocks	3 across x 5 down
Double size	72″ x 90″	20 blocks	4 across x 5 down
Queen size	90″ x 108″	30 blocks	5 across x 6 down
King size	108″ x 108″	36 blocks	6 across x 6 down

METHOD B

Four 12″ square blocks sewn together make one 24″ square block. The blocks referred to in the following chart are, therefore, 24″ squares.

Method B provides for a different quilt measurement—a larger size in each instance. Always check your individual bed size for a happy outcome.

Baby quilt	48" x 48"	4 blocks	2 across x 2 down
Afghan size	48" x 72"	6 blocks	2 across x 3 down
Twin size	72" x 96"	12 blocks	3 across x 4 down
Double size	96" x 96"	16 blocks	4 across x 4 down
King size	120" x 120"	25 blocks	5 across x 5 down

ESTIMATING YARDAGE

Once you determine the number of blocks you will need, fabric must be measured or purchased. If you create blocks from whatever you have in scraps, you will be surprised at how little you'll need for one block. The time will come, of course, when you will want to buy new fabric, and the amounts given here will aid in that purchase. When in doubt, take your templates with you to the fabric store. Lay them on the fabric and determine how much of it you will need for a given block; then multiply by the number of blocks of that design you will be making. Always buy an extra half yard.

Consider, too, the outside treatment (page 90) when purchasing fabric; you may need to purchase an extra yard for bias edging or a ruffle. In some cases, extra backing fabric is needed on the perimeter blocks.

Determine separately the fabric needed to complete each component of your quilt—its blocks, its backing, and, in Method A, its borders. The following tables assume a 45" width fabric.

METHOD A
Block Material

Take the total amount given and divide by the number of fabrics you are using to determine separate yardage for each 12" block.

Baby quilt	6 blocks	1 yard
Afghan size	12 blocks	1½ yards
Twin size	15 blocks	2½ yards
Double size	20 blocks	3½ yards
Queen size	30 blocks	5 yards
King size	36 blocks	5½ yards

Border Material

Fabric needed for the 3"-wide border around each block:

Baby quilt	24 rectangular borders	1½ yards
Afghan size	48 rectangular borders	3 yards
Twin size	60 rectangular borders	3½ yards
Double size	80 rectangular borders	4½ yards
Queen size	120 rectangular borders	7 yards
King size	160 rectangular borders	9 yards

Backing Material

Fabric needed for backing:

Baby quilt	6 blocks	1¾ yards
Afghan size	12 blocks	3½ yards
Twin size	15 blocks	4½ yards
Double size	20 blocks	6 yards
Queen size	30 blocks	9 yards
King size	36 blocks	12 yards

METHOD B

Method B does not call for border yardage since this technique uses block-to-block assembly. It is based on 4 (12") blocks sewn together to make 1 (24") square block.

Block Material

Baby quilt size	16 (12") squares	4 blocks	2 yards
Afghan size	24 (12") squares	6 blocks	4½ yards
Twin size	48 (12") squares	12 blocks	8 yards
Double size	64 (12") squares	16 blocks	12 yards
King size	100 (12") squares	25 blocks	14 yards

Backing Material

Three squares of backing can be cut from every two yards of 45"-wide material. A waste along the sides of 23" will result; this can be used in the front piecework or in another quilt. A striped or print backing can be pieced if you wish to make better use of the material width.

Baby quilt size	3 yards
Afghan size	4½ yards
Twin size	8 yards
Double size	11 yards
King size	16 yards

70 PATCHWORK DESIGNS

The variety of quilt block designs passed on through the years by our foremothers is mind boggling. All of them, though, are based on simple geometric shapes.

Presented here are seventy designs for traditional quilt blocks. The broken lines in the margins show the segments in which the blocks are pieced. In the next chapter, you will find general tips for machine piecing four patch and nine patch blocks, as well as specific tips on a number of these patterns.

Listed beneath each design are the pattern pieces you will need to make them. The patterns themselves appear in the next section of this chapter. All of the shapes are full-sized and include seam allowances and grain lines—all the information you'll need to begin making templates and transferring shapes to fabric.

Keep in mind that the shading in each block is only a suggestion; often, a completely different look can be achieved by switching dark fabric for light, print for dark, etc. And don't be afraid to innovate. Some pattern pieces can be combined to make larger pieces, cutting down on the time it takes to piece a block. The patches of a four patch or even of a nine patch block can be rearranged to form new designs. (This is especially effective when the new design is placed side by side with the original in a quilt.)

If you would like to try your hand at designing new patterns, try cutting pieces out of various colors of construction paper and playing with them as you would with the pieces of a jigsaw puzzle until you find an arrangement that strikes your fancy.

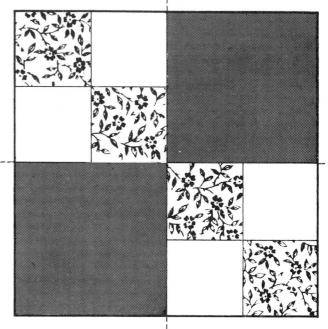

Double Four Patch
2 templates; 10 pieces

Square A	2 dark
Square B	4 light
	4 print

For special tips on machine piecing, see the next chapter.

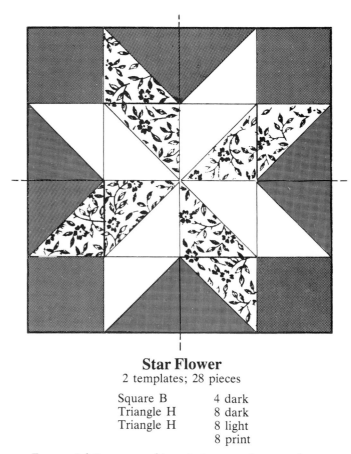

Star Flower
2 templates; 28 pieces

Square B	4 dark
Triangle H	8 dark
Triangle H	8 light
	8 print

For special tips on machine piecing, see the next chapter.

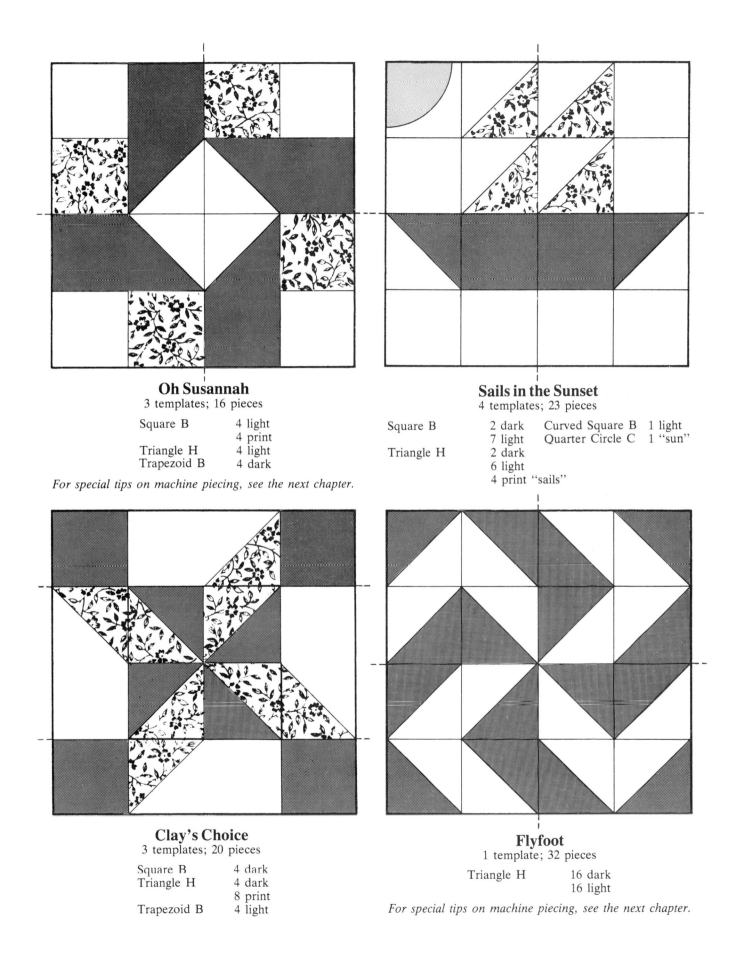

Oh Susannah
3 templates; 16 pieces

Square B	4 light
	4 print
Triangle H	4 light
Trapezoid B	4 dark

For special tips on machine piecing, see the next chapter.

Sails in the Sunset
4 templates; 23 pieces

Square B	2 dark	Curved Square B	1 light
	7 light	Quarter Circle C	1 "sun"
Triangle H	2 dark		
	6 light		
	4 print "sails"		

Clay's Choice
3 templates; 20 pieces

Square B	4 dark
Triangle H	4 dark
	8 print
Trapezoid B	4 light

Flyfoot
1 template; 32 pieces

| Triangle H | 16 dark |
| | 16 light |

For special tips on machine piecing, see the next chapter.

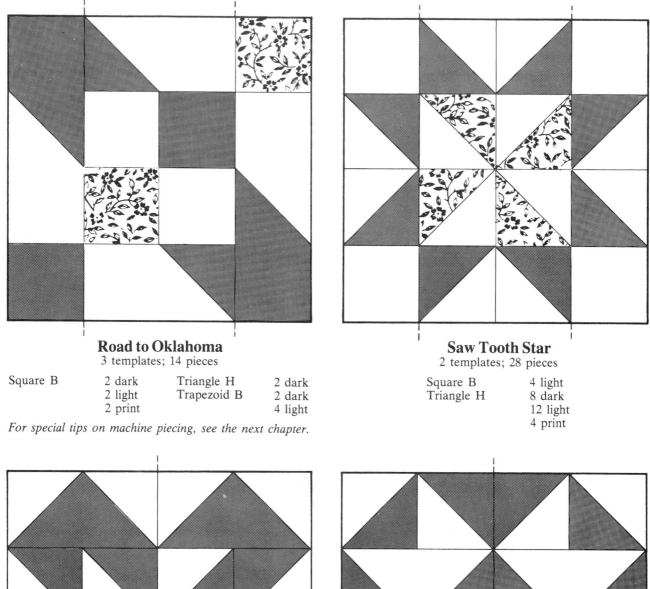

Road to Oklahoma
3 templates; 14 pieces

Square B	2 dark	Triangle H	2 dark
	2 light	Trapezoid B	2 dark
	2 print		4 light

For special tips on machine piecing, see the next chapter.

Saw Tooth Star
2 templates; 28 pieces

Square B	4 light
Triangle H	8 dark
	12 light
	4 print

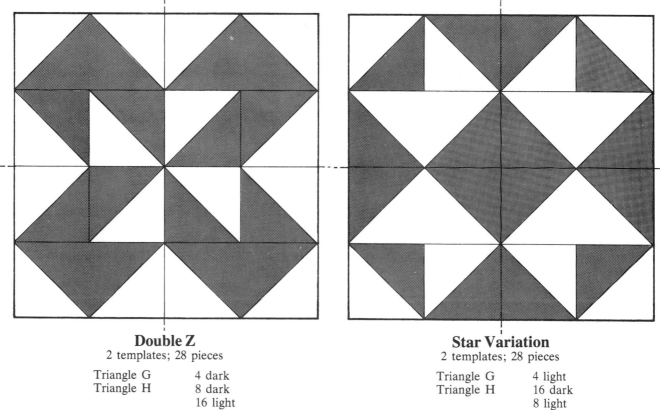

Double Z
2 templates; 28 pieces

Triangle G	4 dark
Triangle H	8 dark
	16 light

For special tips on machine piecing, see the next chapter.

Star Variation
2 templates; 28 pieces

Triangle G	4 light
Triangle H	16 dark
	8 light

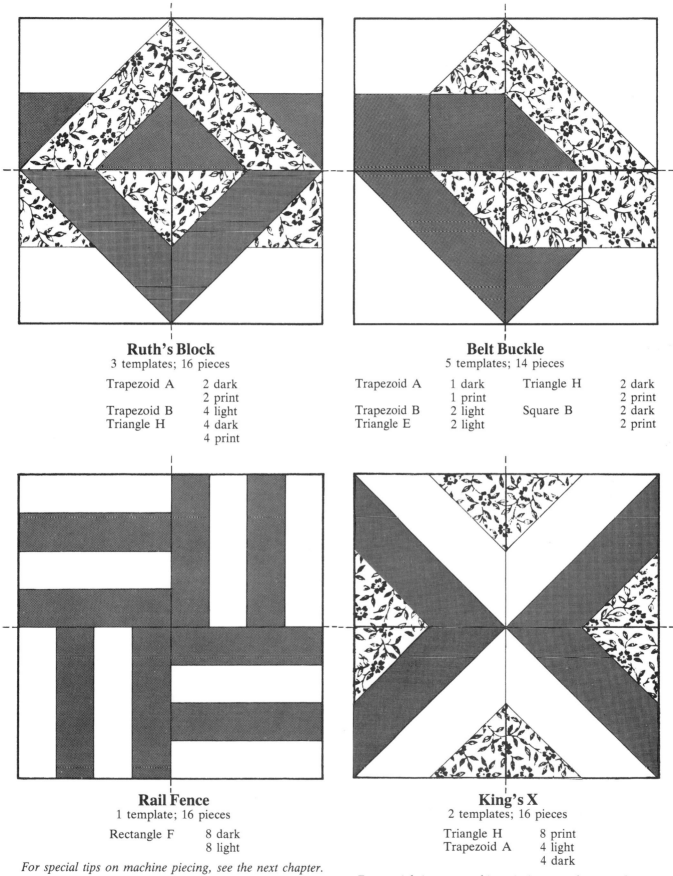

Ruth's Block

3 templates; 16 pieces

Trapezoid A	2 dark
	2 print
Trapezoid B	4 light
Triangle H	4 dark
	4 print

Belt Buckle

5 templates; 14 pieces

Trapezoid A	1 dark	Triangle H	2 dark
	1 print		2 print
Trapezoid B	2 light	Square B	2 dark
Triangle E	2 light		2 print

Rail Fence

1 template; 16 pieces

| Rectangle F | 8 dark |
| | 8 light |

For special tips on machine piecing, see the next chapter.

King's X

2 templates; 16 pieces

Triangle H	8 print
Trapezoid A	4 light
	4 dark

For special tips on machine piecing, see the next chapter.

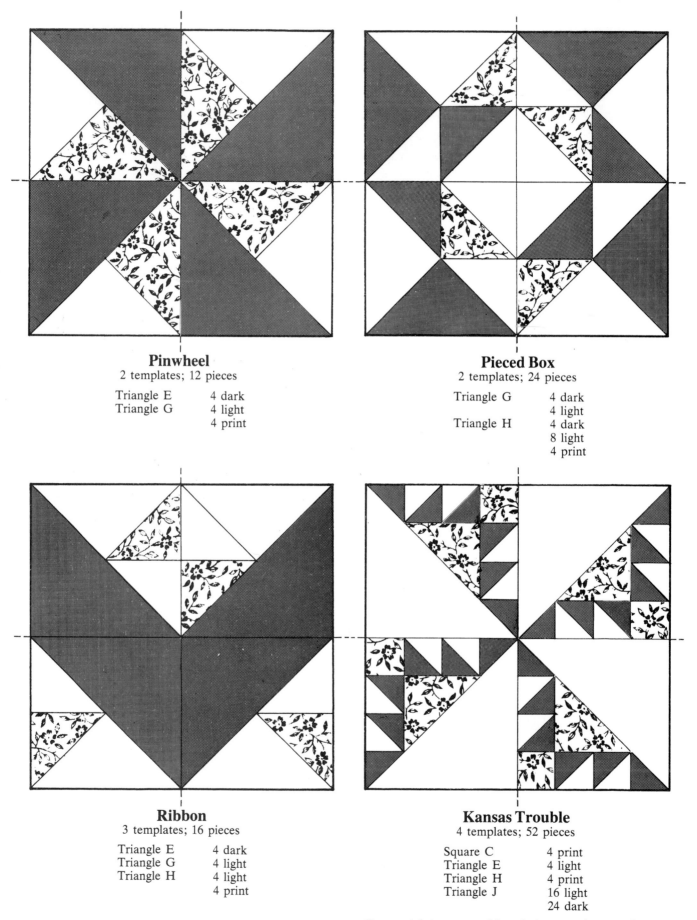

Pinwheel
2 templates; 12 pieces

Triangle E	4 dark
Triangle G	4 light
	4 print

Pieced Box
2 templates; 24 pieces

Triangle G	4 dark
	4 light
Triangle H	4 dark
	8 light
	4 print

Ribbon
3 templates; 16 pieces

Triangle E	4 dark
Triangle G	4 light
Triangle H	4 light
	4 print

Kansas Trouble
4 templates; 52 pieces

Square C	4 print
Triangle E	4 light
Triangle H	4 print
Triangle J	16 light
	24 dark

For special tips on machine piecing, see the next chapter.

Drunkard's Path
2 templates; 8 pieces

Curved Square A	2 dark
	2 light
Quarter Circle A	2 dark
	2 light

For special tips on machine piecing, see the next chapter.

Love Ring
2 templates; 32 pieces

Curved Square B	8 light
	8 dark
Quarter Circle C	8 dark
	8 light

Coffee Cup
7 templates; 21 pieces

Square B	2 dark	Triangle J	2 dark
	4 light		4 light
Square C	2 light	Pentagon B	2 dark
Rectangle F	1 dark	Rectangle L	1 light
	2 light	Handle A	1 dark
		Appliqué the handle.	

For special tips on machine piecing, see the next chapter.

Combo Block
4 templates; 28 pieces

Square B	4 dark
Triangle H	4 light
	4 print
Curved Square B	8 light
Quarter Circle C	8 dark

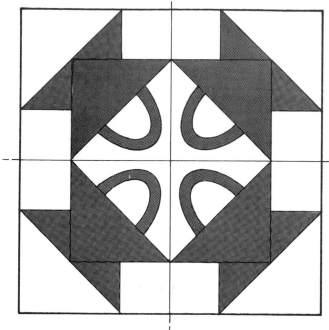

Postage Stamp Basket
4 templates; 32 pieces

Square G	8 light	Triangle I	8 dark
Triangle A	4 dark	Handle B	4 dark
	8 light	Appliqué the handle.	

Checkerboard
1 template; 64 pieces

Square C	32 dark
	32 light

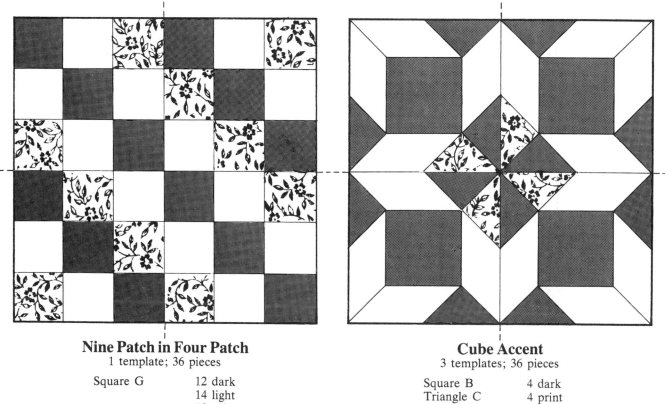

Nine Patch in Four Patch
1 template; 36 pieces

Square G	12 dark
	14 light
	10 print

Cube Accent
3 templates; 36 pieces

Square B	4 dark
Triangle C	4 print
	12 dark
Parallelogram C	16 light*

*Cut 8; then flop template to cut remaining 8.

For special tips on machine piecing, see the next chapter.

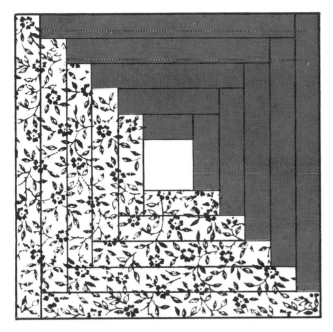

Log Cabin
2 templates; 21 pieces

Square G	1 light
Rectangle B	2½ yards dark
	2½ yards print

Add strips in a clockwise direction.

For special tips on machine piecing, see the next chapter.

Log Cabin Variation #1
2 templates; 21 pieces

Square G	1 light
Rectangle B	2½ yards dark
	2½ yards print

Add strips in a clockwise direction.

For special tips on machine piecing, see the next chapter.

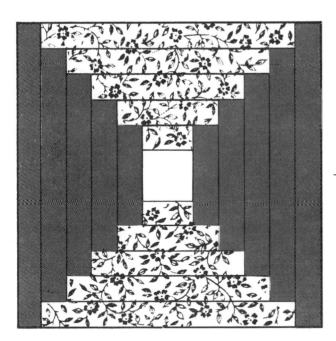

Log Cabin Variation #2
2 templates; 21 pieces

Square G	1 light
Rectangle B	2½ yards dark
	2½ yards print

Add strips in a clockwise direction.

For special tips on machine piecing, see the next chapter.

Log Cabin Four Patch
2 templates; 36 pieces

Square G	4 light
Rectangle B	2½ yards dark
	2½ yards print

Add strips in a clockwise direction.

For special tips on machine piecing, see the next chapter.

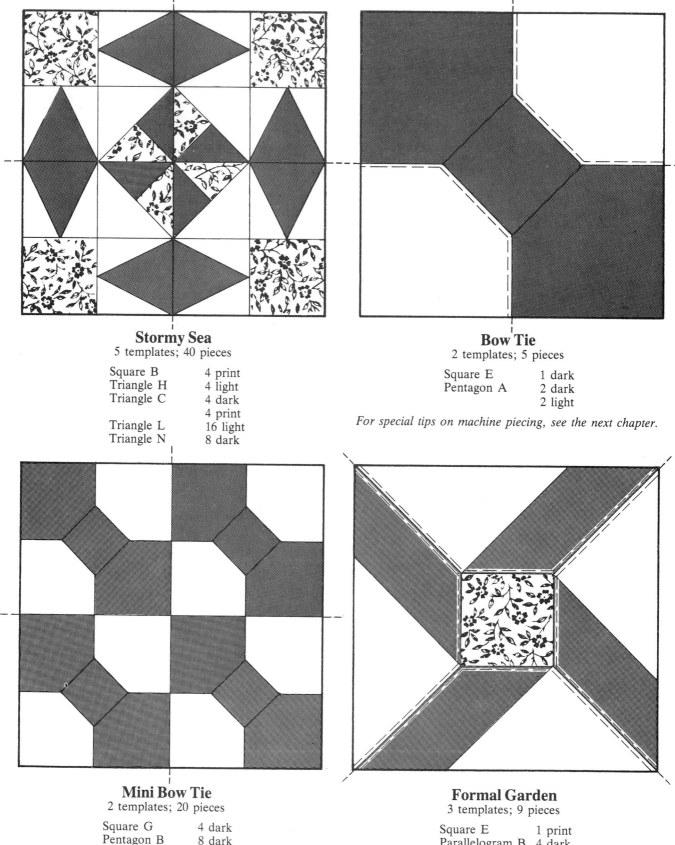

Stormy Sea
5 templates; 40 pieces

Square B	4 print
Triangle H	4 light
Triangle C	4 dark
	4 print
Triangle L	16 light
Triangle N	8 dark

Bow Tie
2 templates; 5 pieces

Square E	1 dark
Pentagon A	2 dark
	2 light

For special tips on machine piecing, see the next chapter.

Mini Bow Tie
2 templates; 20 pieces

Square G	4 dark
Pentagon B	8 dark
	8 light

Formal Garden
3 templates; 9 pieces

Square E	1 print
Parallelogram B	4 dark
Triangle S	4 light

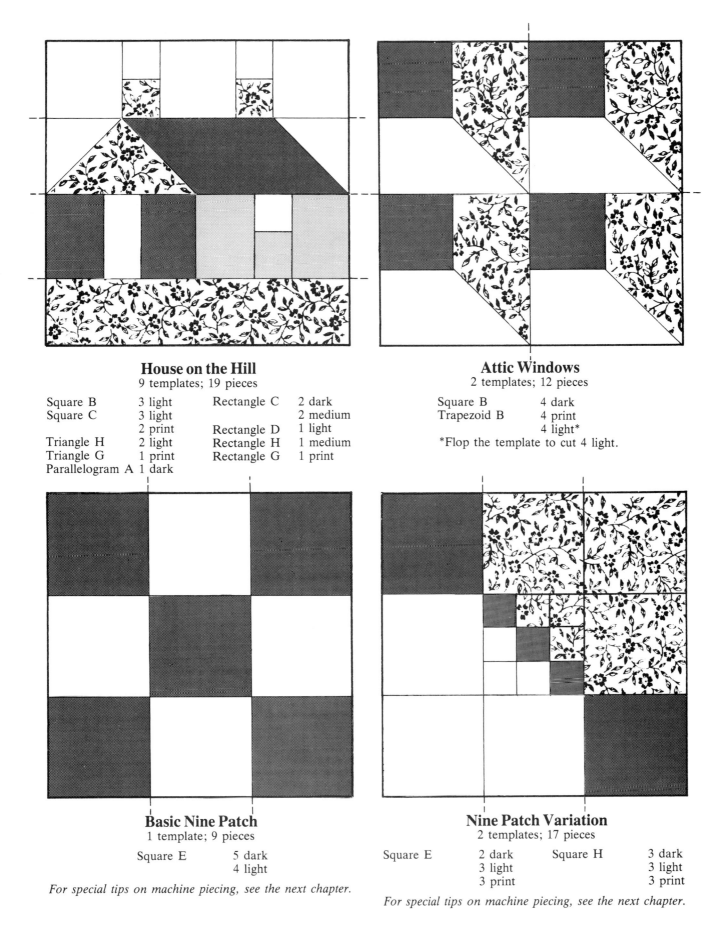

House on the Hill
9 templates; 19 pieces

Square B	3 light	Rectangle C	2 dark
Square C	3 light		2 medium
	2 print	Rectangle D	1 light
Triangle H	2 light	Rectangle H	1 medium
Triangle G	1 print	Rectangle G	1 print
Parallelogram A	1 dark		

Attic Windows
2 templates; 12 pieces

Square B	4 dark
Trapezoid B	4 print
	4 light*

*Flop the template to cut 4 light.

Basic Nine Patch
1 template; 9 pieces

Square E	5 dark
	4 light

For special tips on machine piecing, see the next chapter.

Nine Patch Variation
2 templates; 17 pieces

Square E	2 dark	Square H	3 dark
	3 light		3 light
	3 print		3 print

For special tips on machine piecing, see the next chapter.

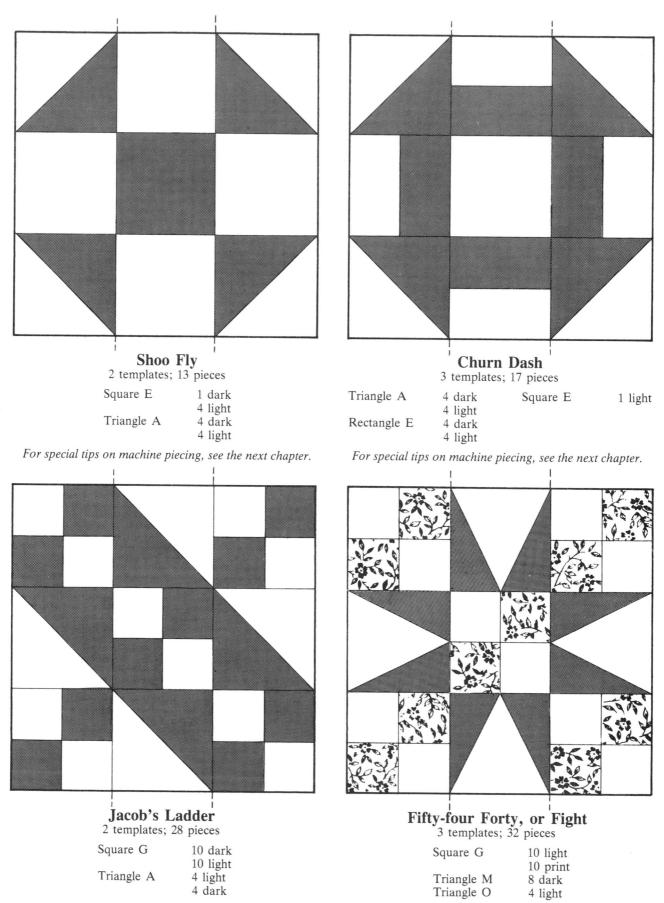

Shoo Fly
2 templates; 13 pieces

Square E	1 dark	
	4 light	
Triangle A	4 dark	
	4 light	

For special tips on machine piecing, see the next chapter.

Churn Dash
3 templates; 17 pieces

Triangle A	4 dark	Square E	1 light
	4 light		
Rectangle E	4 dark		
	4 light		

For special tips on machine piecing, see the next chapter.

Jacob's Ladder
2 templates; 28 pieces

Square G	10 dark
	10 light
Triangle A	4 light
	4 dark

For special tips on machine piecing, see the next chapter.

Fifty-four Forty, or Fight
3 templates; 32 pieces

Square G	10 light
	10 print
Triangle M	8 dark
Triangle O	4 light

For special tips on machine piecing, see the next chapter.

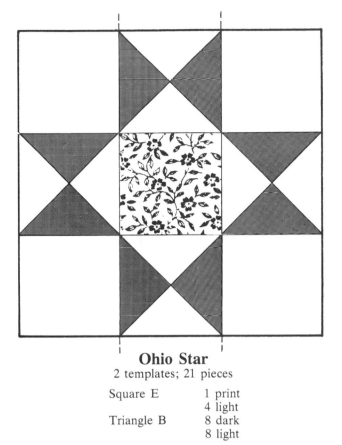

Ohio Star
2 templates; 21 pieces

Square E	1 print
	4 light
Triangle B	8 dark
	8 light

For special tips on machine piecing, see the next chapter.

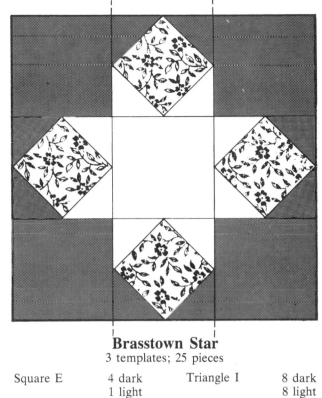

Brasstown Star
3 templates; 25 pieces

Square E	4 dark	Triangle I	8 dark
	1 light		8 light
Square I	4 print		

For special tips on machine piecing, see the next chapter.

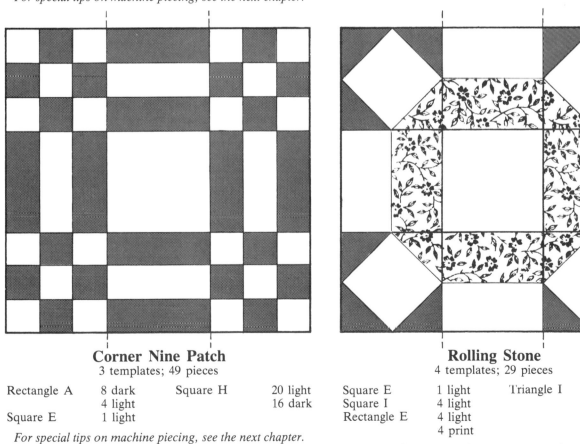

Corner Nine Patch
3 templates; 49 pieces

Rectangle A	8 dark	Square H	20 light
	4 light		16 dark
Square E	1 light		

For special tips on machine piecing, see the next chapter.

Rolling Stone
4 templates; 29 pieces

Square E	1 light	Triangle I	12 dark
Square I	4 light		4 print
Rectangle E	4 light		
	4 print		

For special tips on machine piecing, see the next chapter.

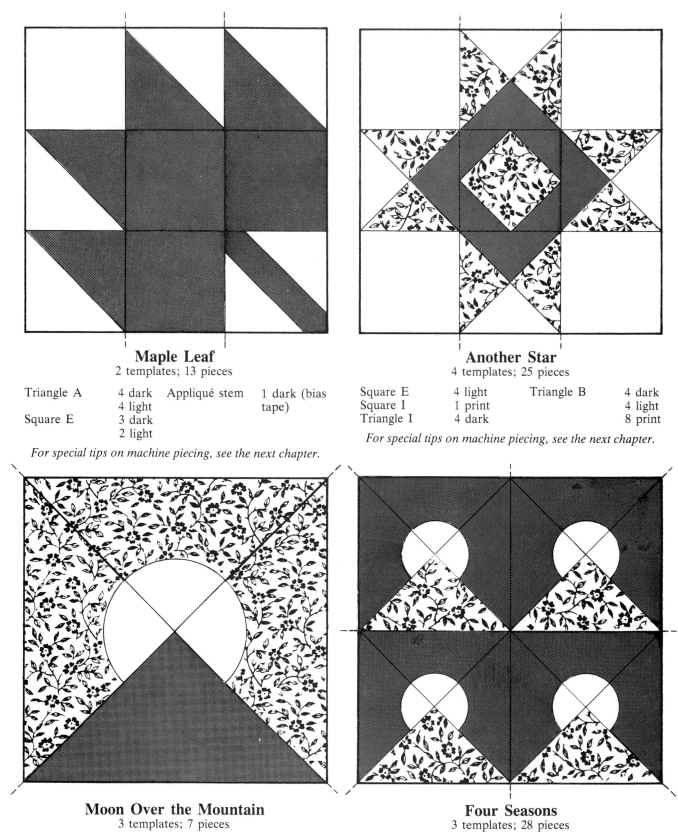

Maple Leaf
2 templates; 13 pieces

Triangle A	4 dark	Appliqué stem	1 dark (bias
	4 light		tape)
Square E	3 dark		
	2 light		

For special tips on machine piecing, see the next chapter.

Another Star
4 templates; 25 pieces

Square E	4 light	Triangle B	4 dark
Square I	1 print		4 light
Triangle I	4 dark		8 print

For special tips on machine piecing, see the next chapter.

Moon Over the Mountain
3 templates; 7 pieces

Moon Mountain	1 dark
Moon Sky	3 print
Quarter Circle B	3 light

For special tips on machine piecing, see the next chapter.

Four Seasons
3 templates; 28 pieces

Triangle G	4 print
Four Seasons Sky	12 dark
Quarter Circle D	12 light

For special tips on machine piecing, see the next chapter.

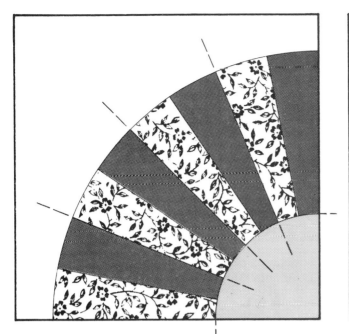

Grandmother's Fan
2 templates; 9 pieces

Quarter Circle A   1 dark
Fan Wedge   8 different prints
Appliqué on a 12½″ square.

For special tips on machine piecing, see the next chapter.

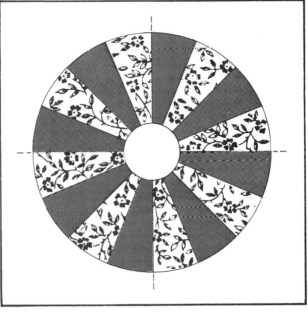

Dresden Plate
2 templates; 17 pieces

Plate Circle   1 light
Plate Wedge   8 dark and 8 print
                 or 16 different prints
Appliqué on a 12½ square.

For special tips on machine piecing, see the next chapter.

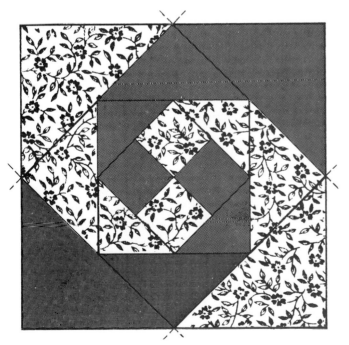

Monkey Wrench
4 templates; 16 pieces

Square D	2 dark	Triangle G	2 dark
	2 print		2 print
Triangle E	2 dark	Triangle H	2 dark
	2 print		2 print

For special tips on machine piecing, see the next chapter.

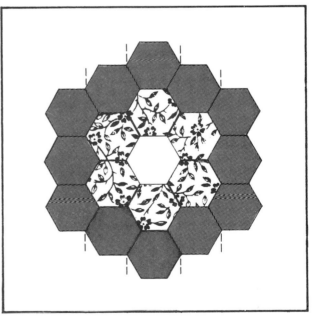

Hexagon Flowerette
1 template; 19 pieces

Hexagon   1 light
            6 print
            12 dark
Appliqué on a 12½ square.

For special tips on machine piecing, see the next chapter.

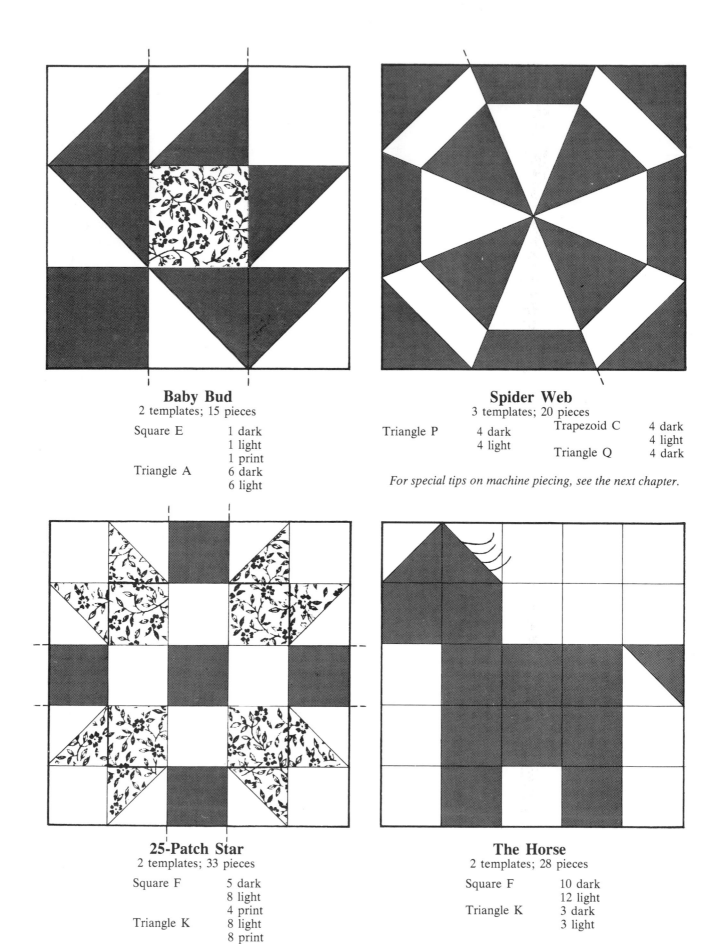

Baby Bud

2 templates; 15 pieces

Square E	1 dark
	1 light
	1 print
Triangle A	6 dark
	6 light

Spider Web

3 templates; 20 pieces

Triangle P	4 dark	Trapezoid C	4 dark
	4 light		4 light
		Triangle Q	4 dark

For special tips on machine piecing, see the next chapter.

25-Patch Star

2 templates; 33 pieces

Square F	5 dark
	8 light
	4 print
Triangle K	8 light
	8 print

The Horse

2 templates; 28 pieces

Square F	10 dark
	12 light
Triangle K	3 dark
	3 light

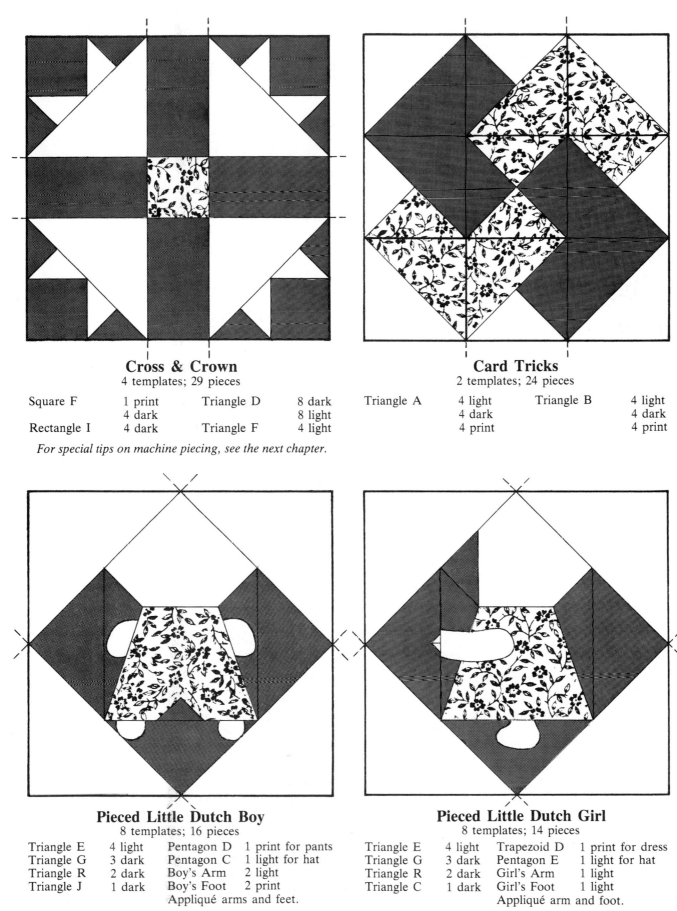

Cross & Crown
4 templates; 29 pieces

Square F	1 print	Triangle D	8 dark
	4 dark		8 light
Rectangle I	4 dark	Triangle F	4 light

For special tips on machine piecing, see the next chapter.

Card Tricks
2 templates; 24 pieces

Triangle A	4 light	Triangle B	4 light
	4 dark		4 dark
	4 print		4 print

Pieced Little Dutch Boy
8 templates; 16 pieces

Triangle E	4 light	Pentagon D	1 print for pants
Triangle G	3 dark	Pentagon C	1 light for hat
Triangle R	2 dark	Boy's Arm	2 light
Triangle J	1 dark	Boy's Foot	2 print
		Appliqué arms and feet.	

For special tips on machine piecing, see the next chapter.

Pieced Little Dutch Girl
8 templates; 14 pieces

Triangle E	4 light	Trapezoid D	1 print for dress
Triangle G	3 dark	Pentagon E	1 light for hat
Triangle R	2 dark	Girl's Arm	1 light
Triangle C	1 dark	Girl's Foot	1 light
		Appliqué arm and foot.	

For special tips on machine piecing, see the next chapter.

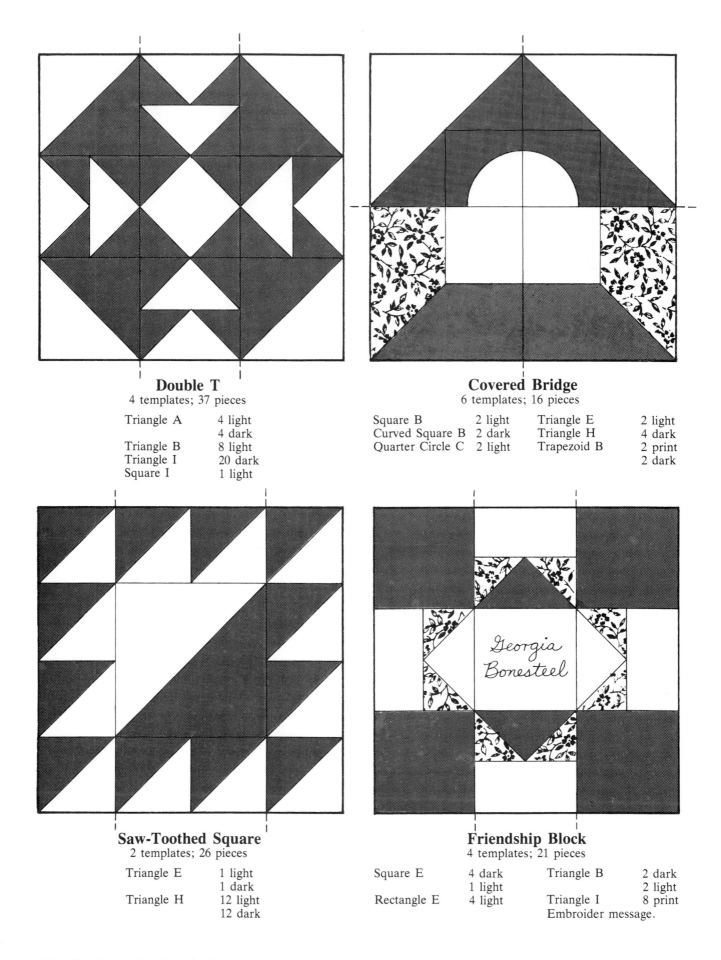

Double T
4 templates; 37 pieces

Triangle A	4 light
	4 dark
Triangle B	8 light
Triangle I	20 dark
Square I	1 light

Covered Bridge
6 templates; 16 pieces

Square B	2 light	Triangle E	2 light
Curved Square B	2 dark	Triangle H	4 dark
Quarter Circle C	2 light	Trapezoid B	2 print
			2 dark

Saw-Toothed Square
2 templates; 26 pieces

Triangle E	1 light
	1 dark
Triangle H	12 light
	12 dark

Friendship Block
4 templates; 21 pieces

Square E	4 dark	Triangle B	2 dark
	1 light		2 light
Rectangle E	4 light	Triangle I	8 print
		Embroider message.	

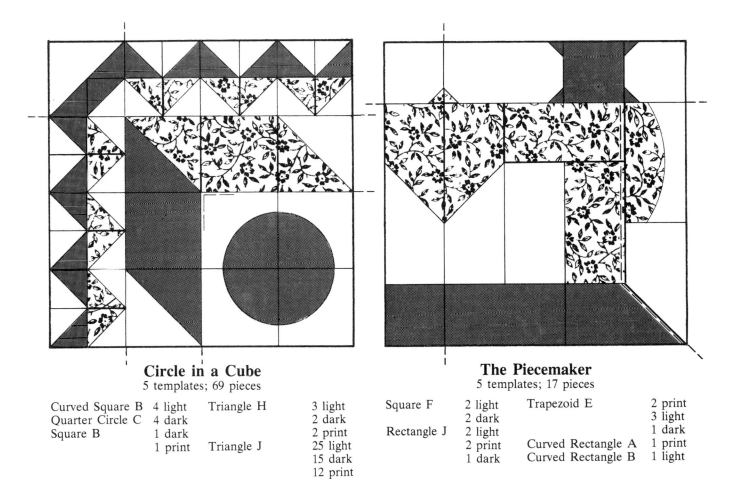

Circle in a Cube
5 templates; 69 pieces

Curved Square B	4 light	Triangle H	3 light
Quarter Circle C	4 dark		2 dark
Square B	1 dark		2 print
	1 print	Triangle J	25 light
			15 dark
			12 print

The Piecemaker
5 templates; 17 pieces

Square F	2 light	Trapezoid E	2 print
	2 dark		3 light
Rectangle J	2 light		1 dark
	2 print	Curved Rectangle A	1 print
	1 dark	Curved Rectangle B	1 light

Rooster
4 templates; 4 pieces

Rooster	1 dark
Tailfeathers	3 different prints

Appliqué on a 12½″ square.

Morning Glory
6 templates; 6 pieces

Morning Glory A-F
Appliqué on a 12 ½″ square.

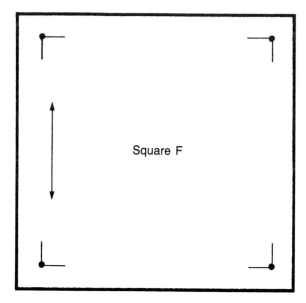

Square F

PATTERNS FOR TEMPLATES

These full-sized patterns include all the shapes you will need to piece together any of the designs in this book. Their names correspond to the shapes listed under the individual designs. Arrows are grain lines.

Be sure to read the section on making templates in the next chapter for advice on how to use these patterns. Remember that each of these patterns includes a ¼″ seam allowance and the lines therefore represent the cutting edge of the fabric.

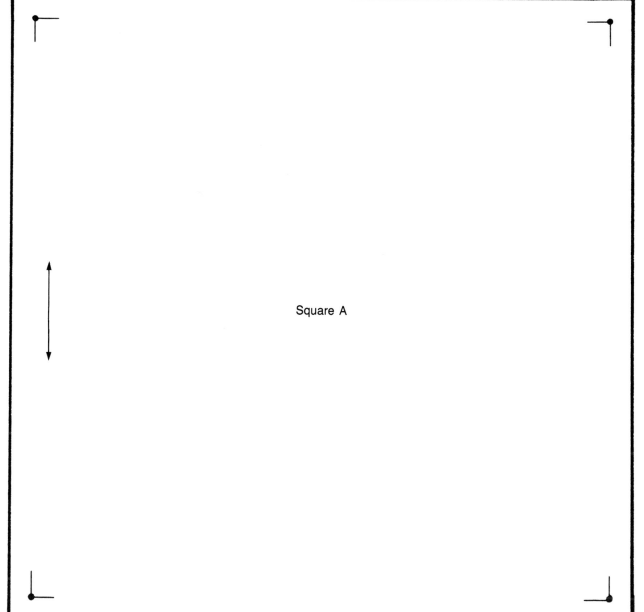

Square A

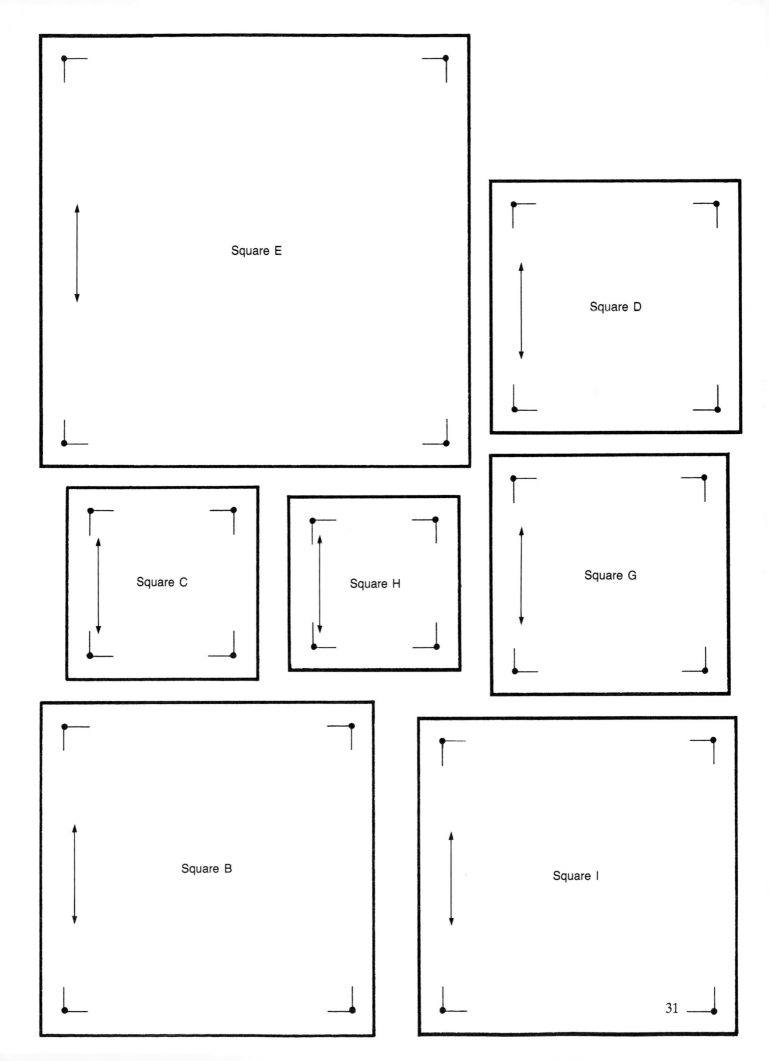

Square E

Square D

Square C

Square H

Square G

Square B

Square I

31

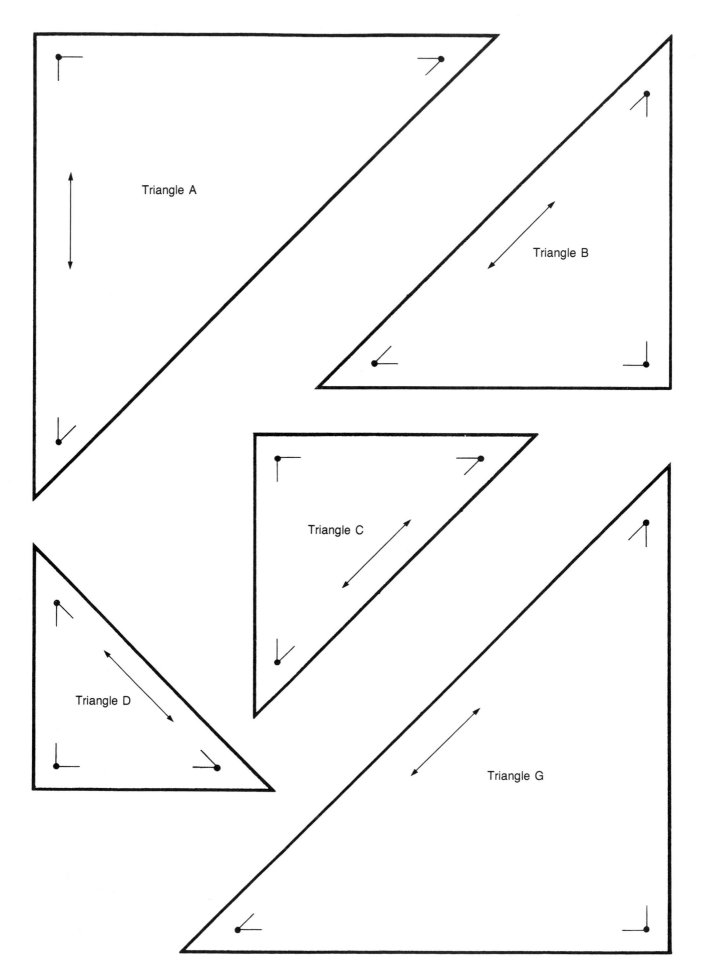

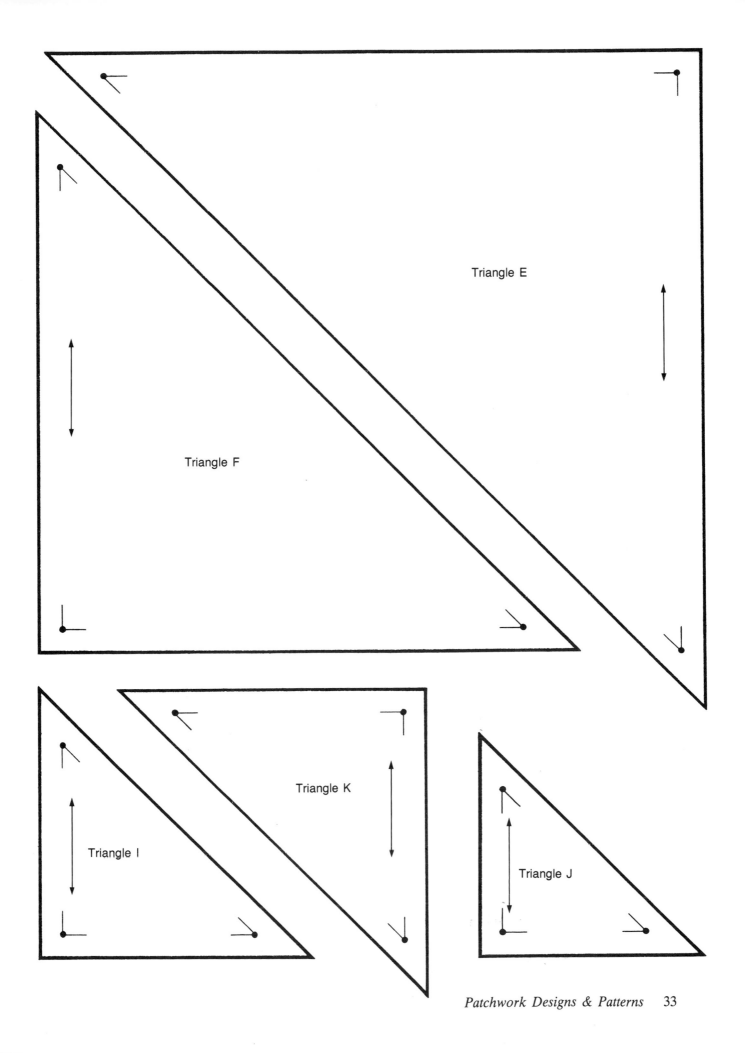

Triangle E

Triangle F

Triangle K

Triangle I

Triangle J

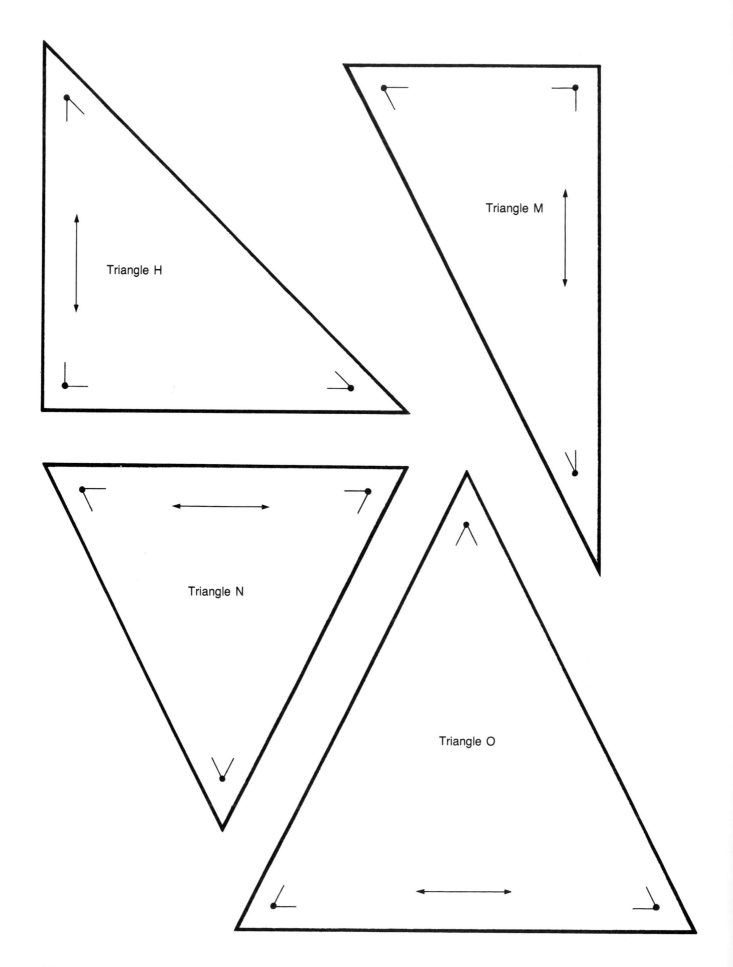

Triangle H

Triangle M

Triangle N

Triangle O

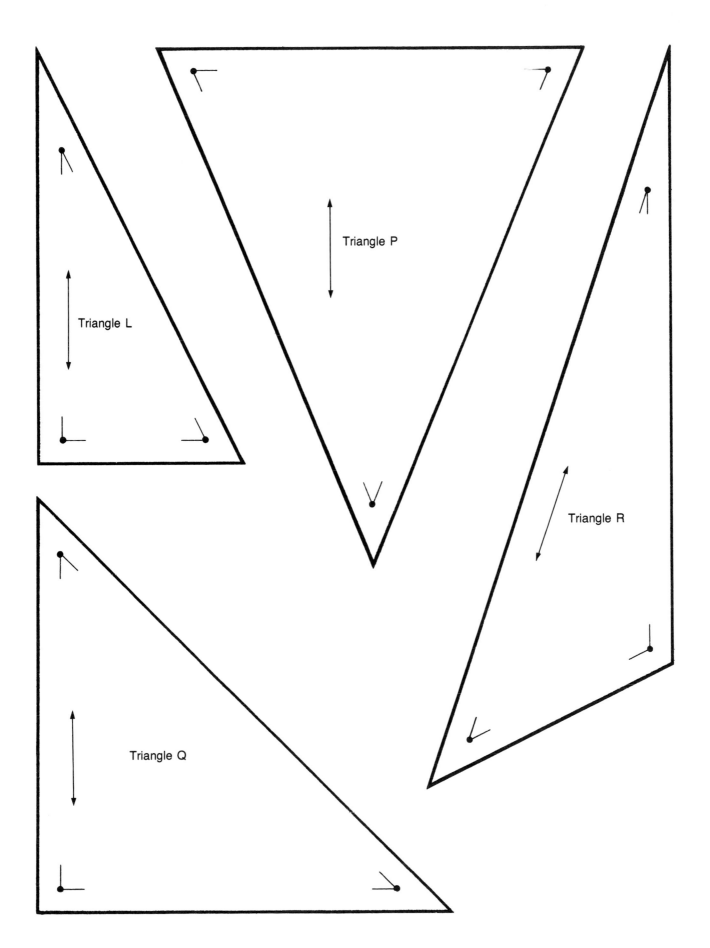

Triangle P

Triangle L

Triangle R

Triangle Q

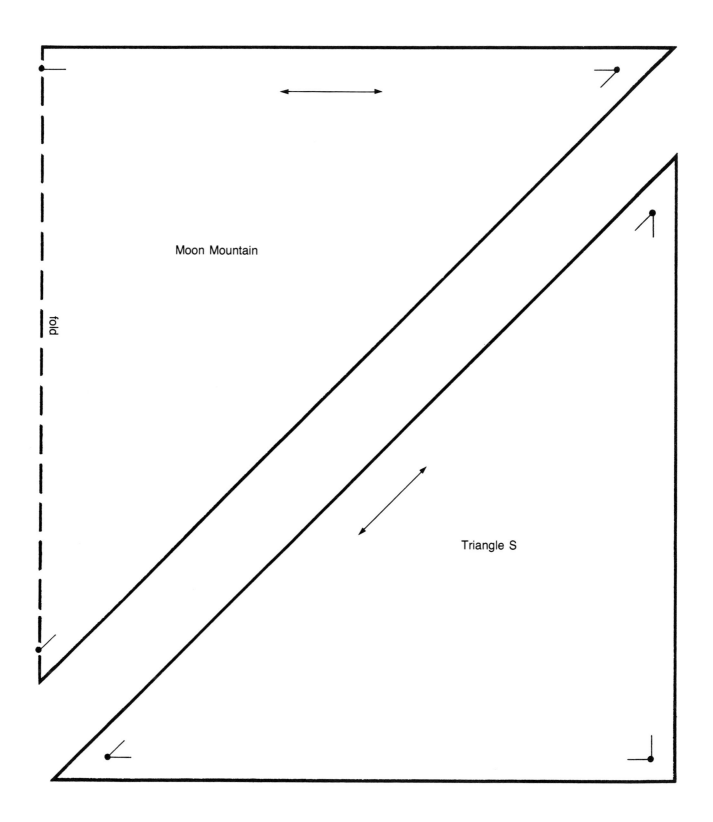

Moon Mountain

fold

Triangle S

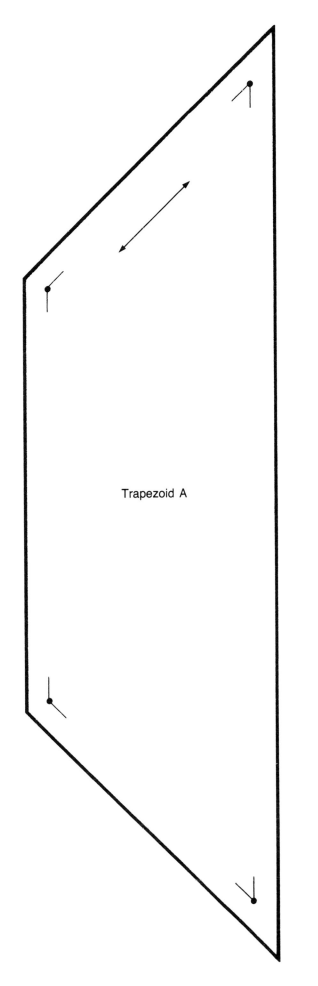

Trapezoid A

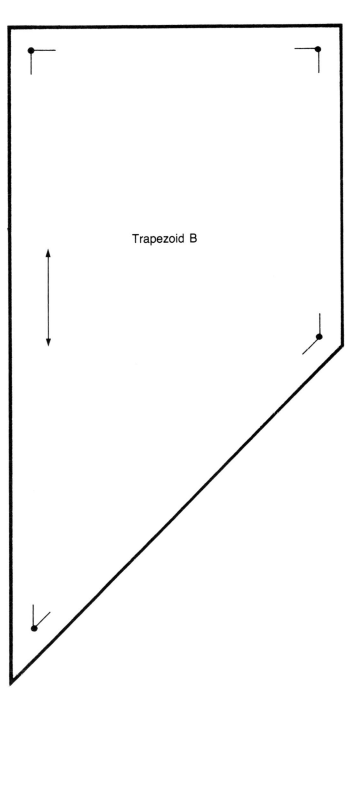

Trapezoid B

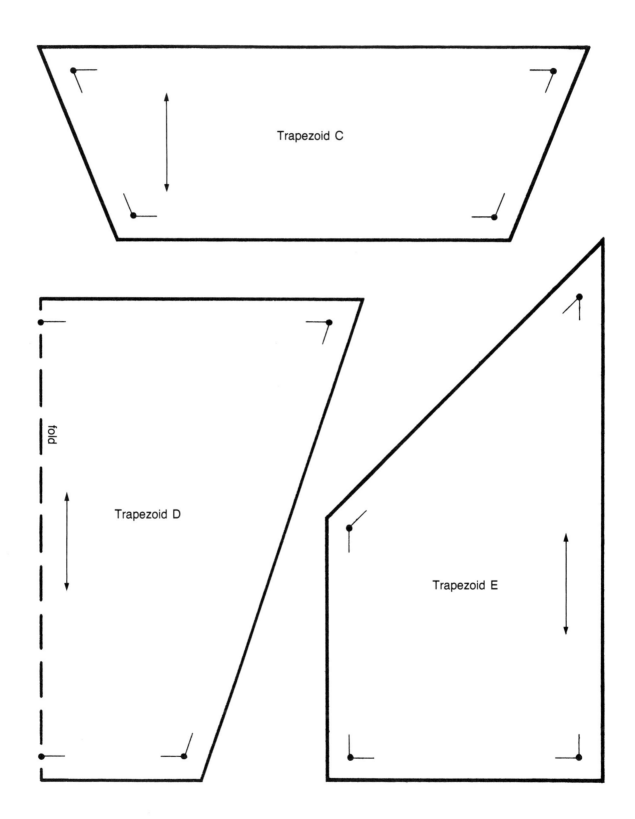

Trapezoid C

fold

Trapezoid D

Trapezoid E

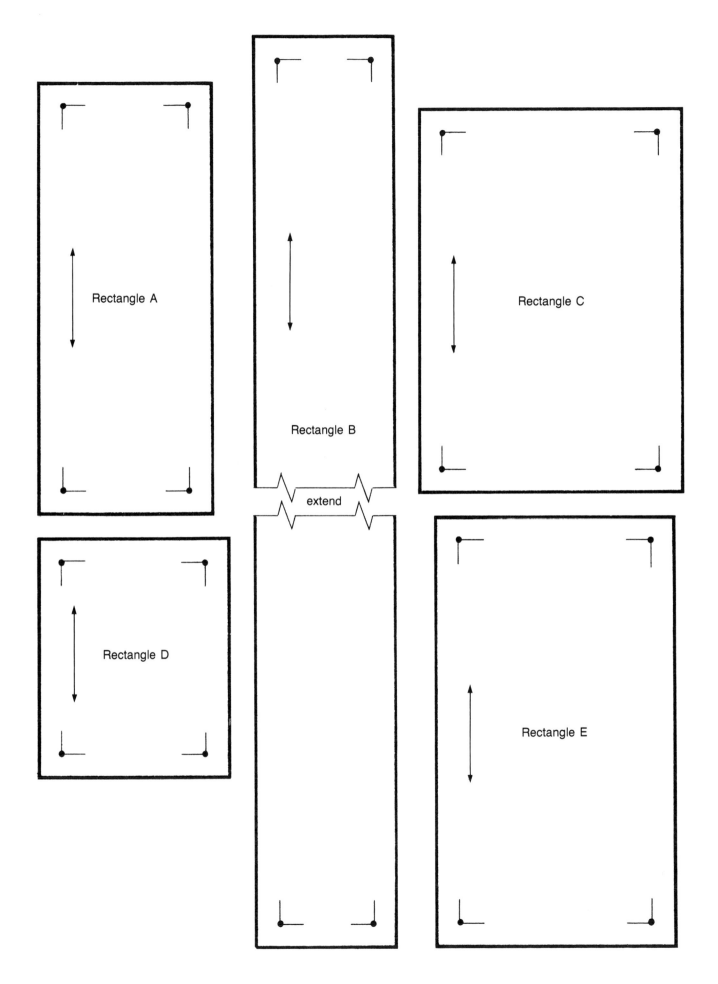

Rectangle A

Rectangle B

Rectangle C

extend

Rectangle D

Rectangle E

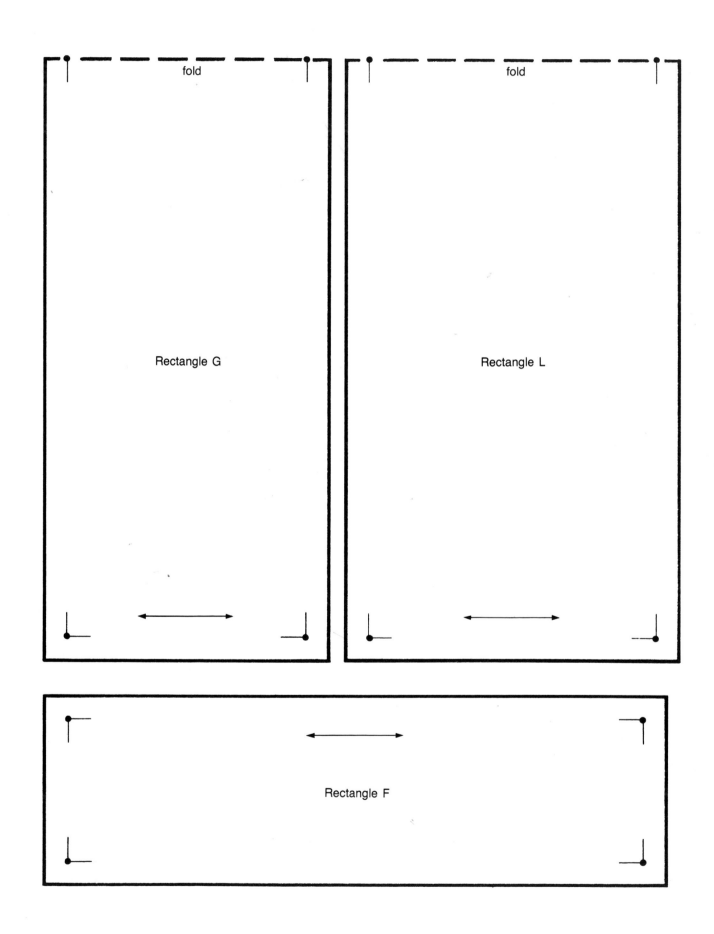

fold

Rectangle G

fold

Rectangle L

Rectangle F

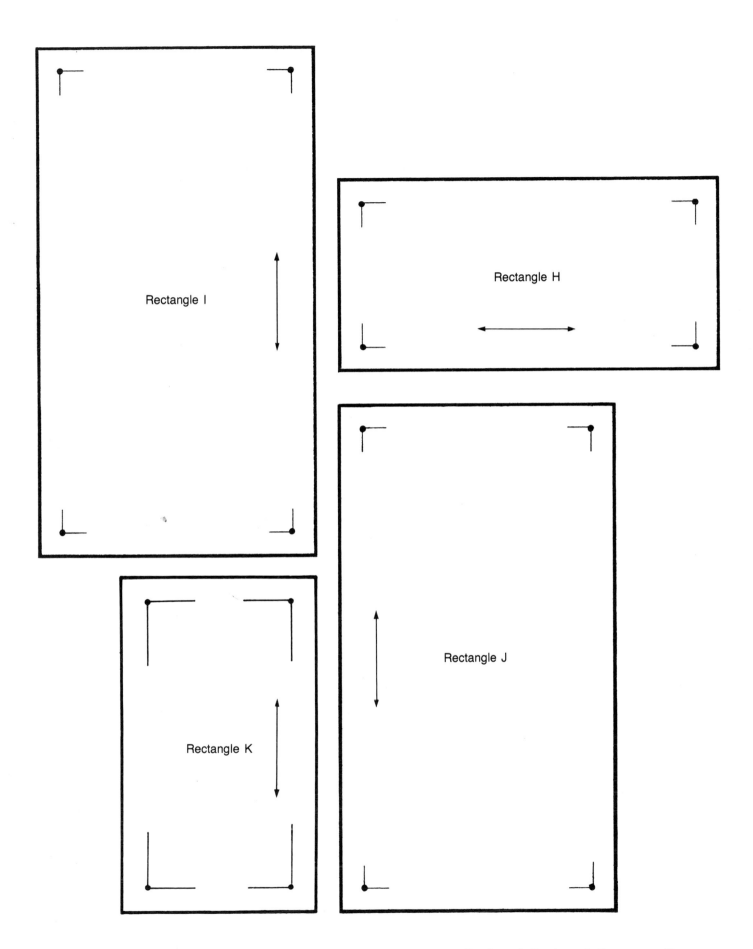

Rectangle I

Rectangle H

Rectangle J

Rectangle K

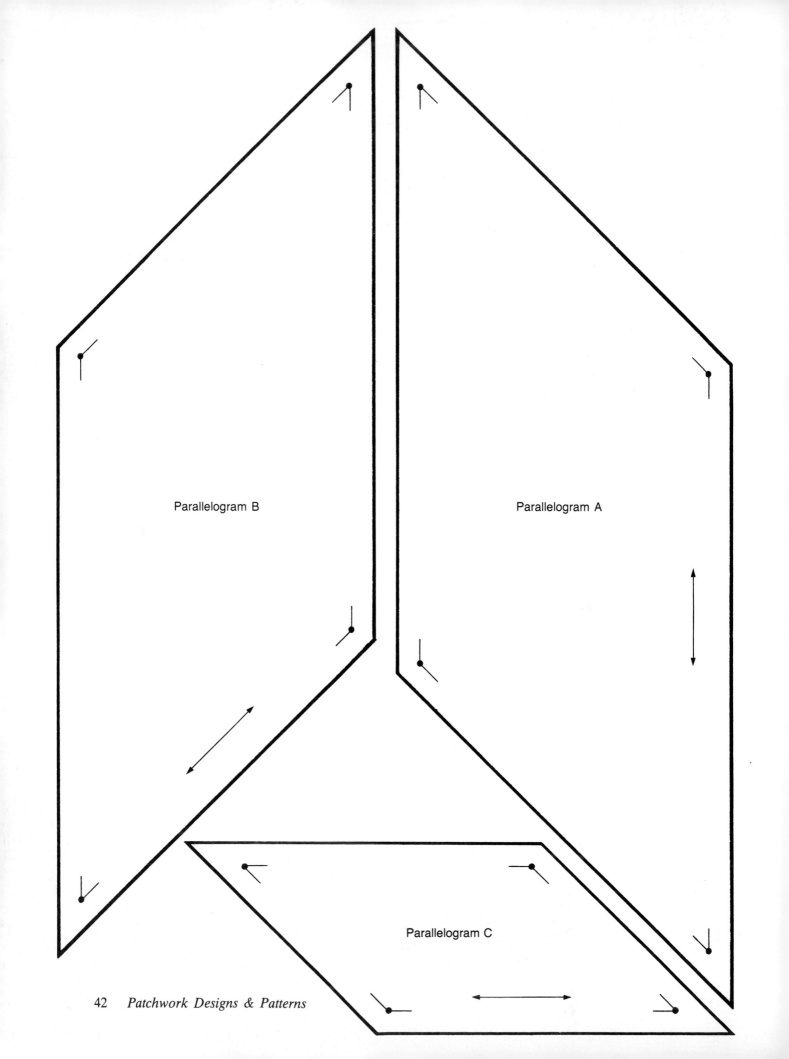

Parallelogram B

Parallelogram A

Parallelogram C

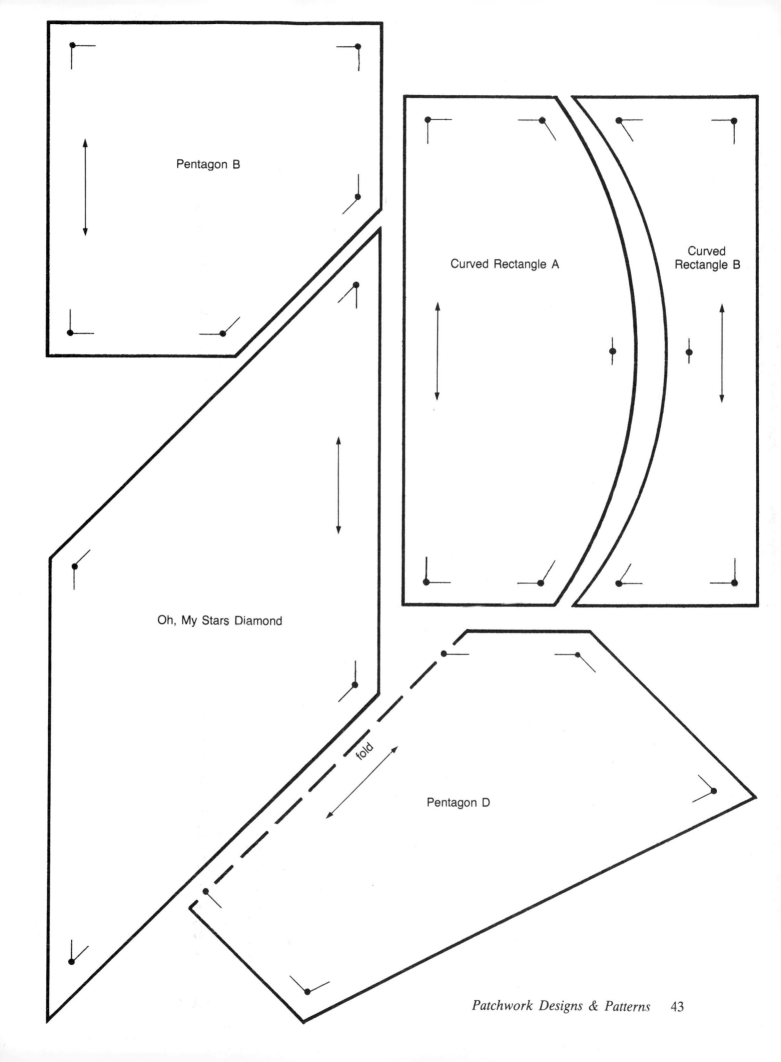

Pentagon B

Curved Rectangle A

Curved Rectangle B

Oh, My Stars Diamond

fold

Pentagon D

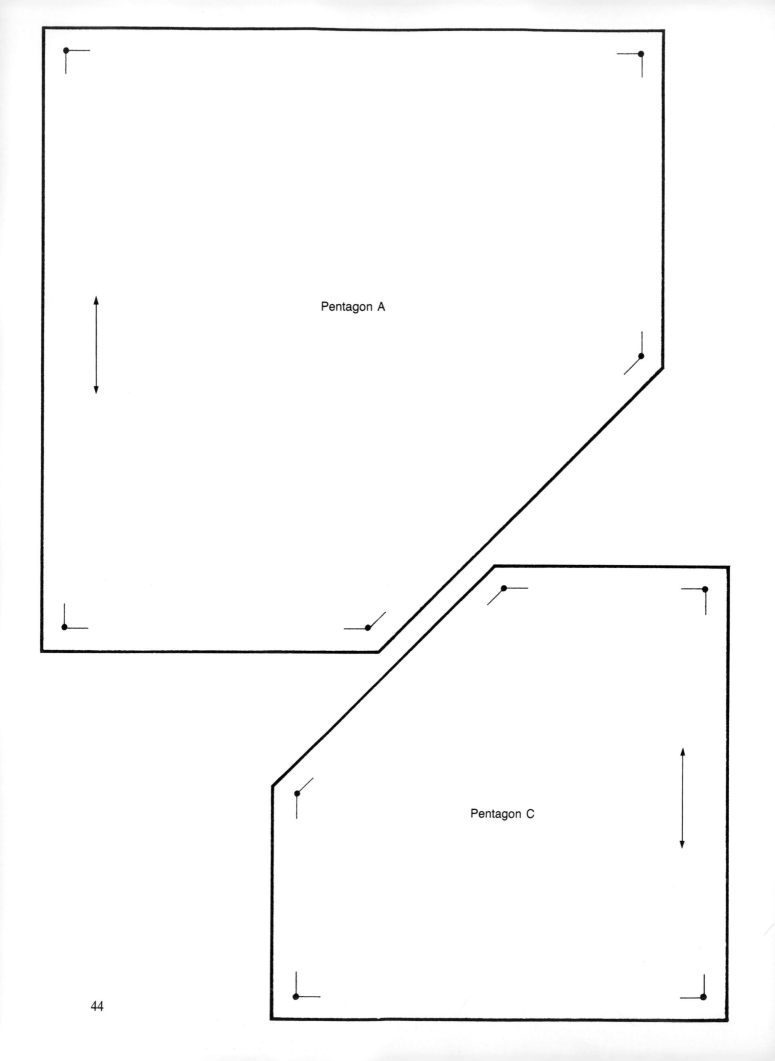

Pentagon A

Pentagon C

44

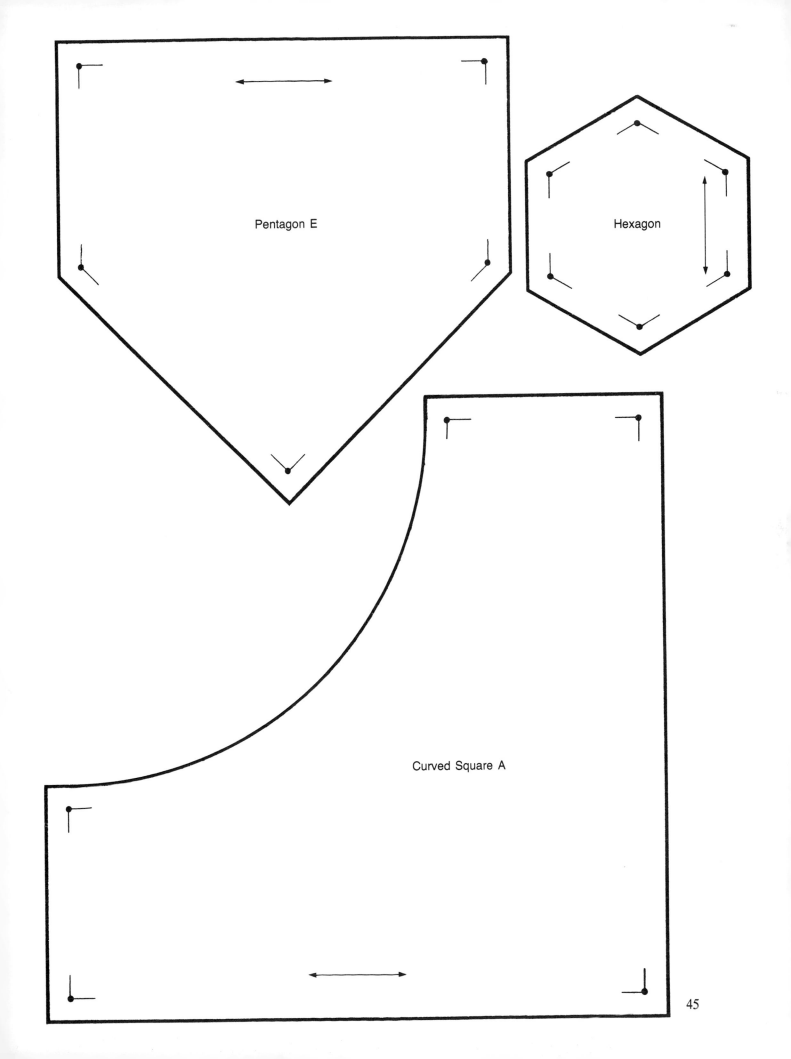

Pentagon E

Hexagon

Curved Square A

45

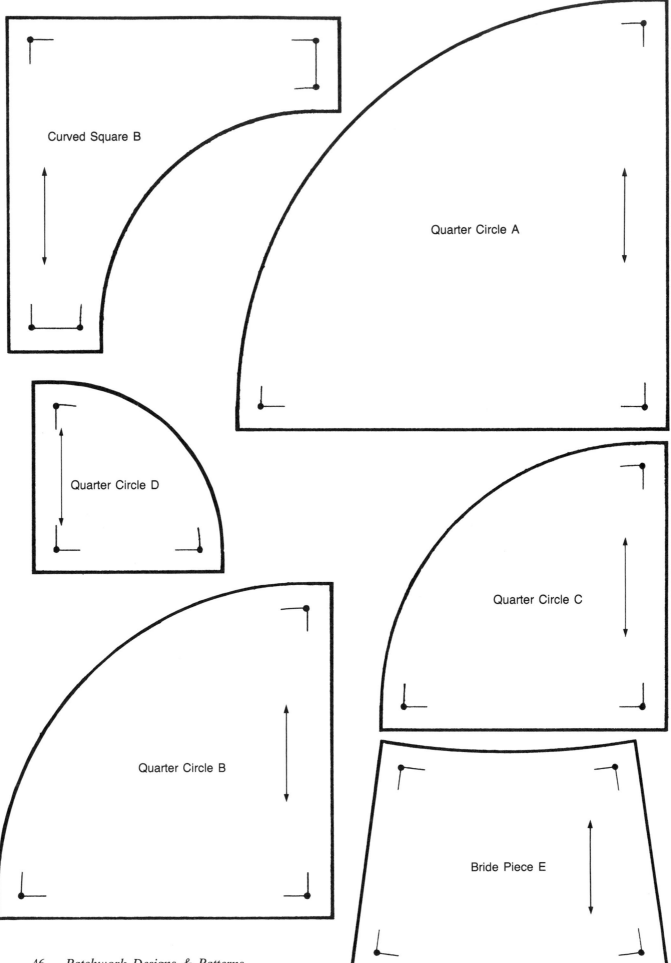

Curved Square B

Quarter Circle A

Quarter Circle D

Quarter Circle C

Quarter Circle B

Bride Piece E

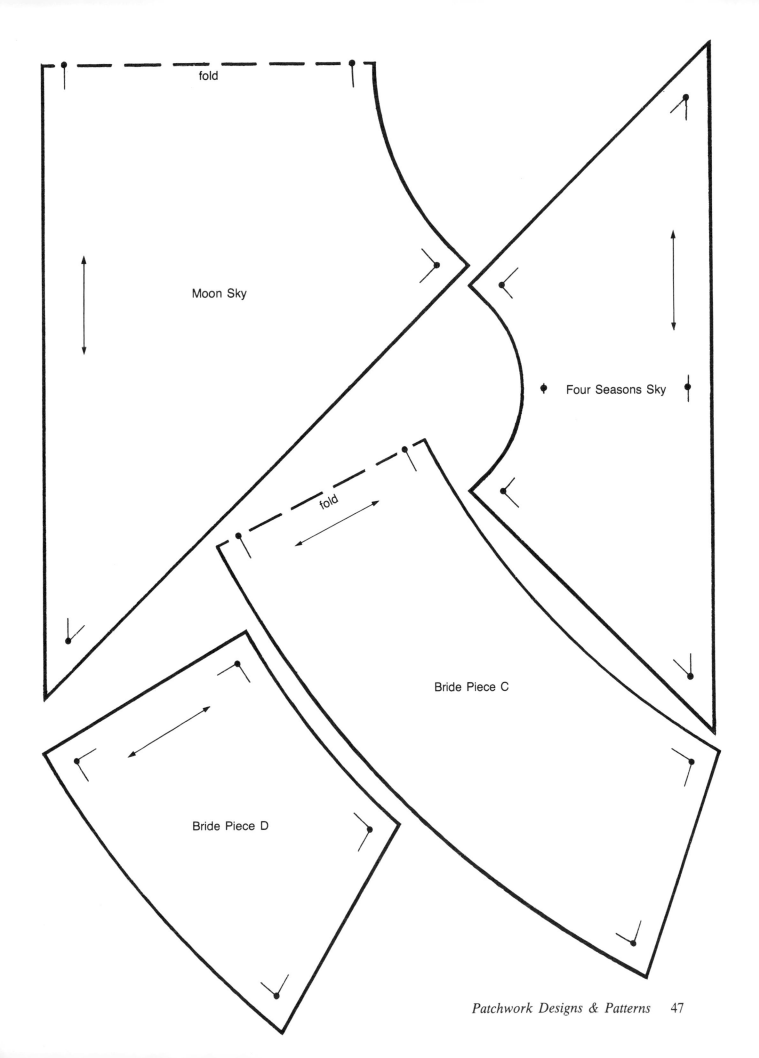

fold

Moon Sky

Four Seasons Sky

fold

Bride Piece C

Bride Piece D

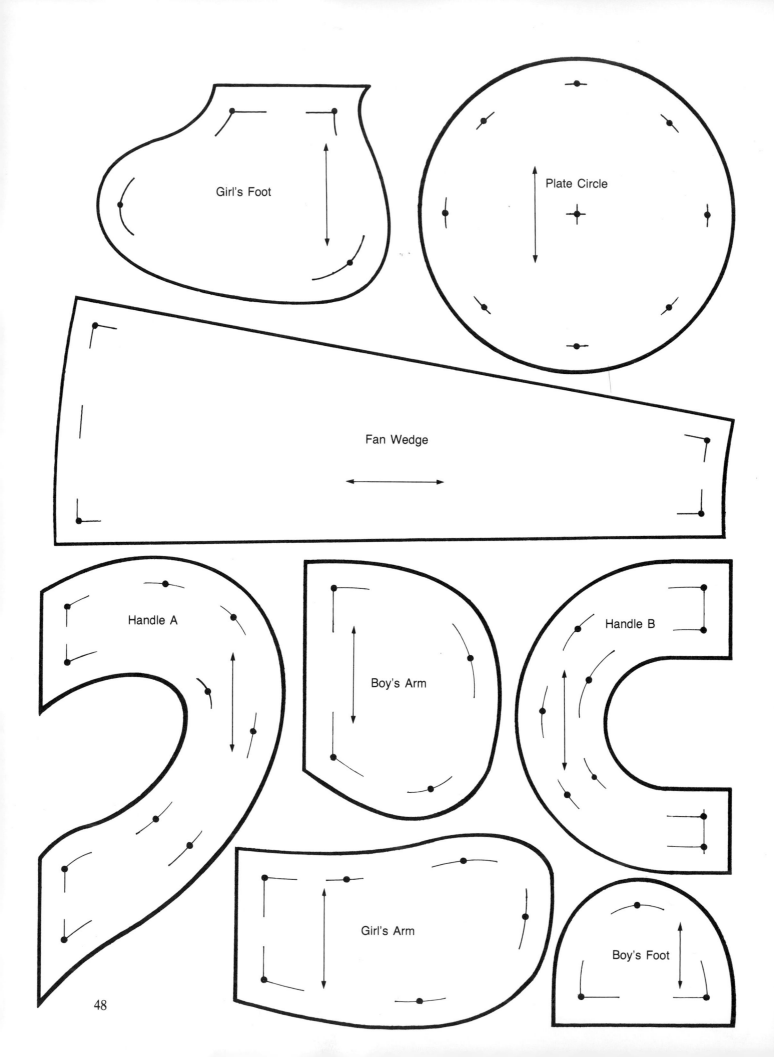

Girl's Foot

Plate Circle

Fan Wedge

Handle A

Boy's Arm

Handle B

Girl's Arm

Boy's Foot

48

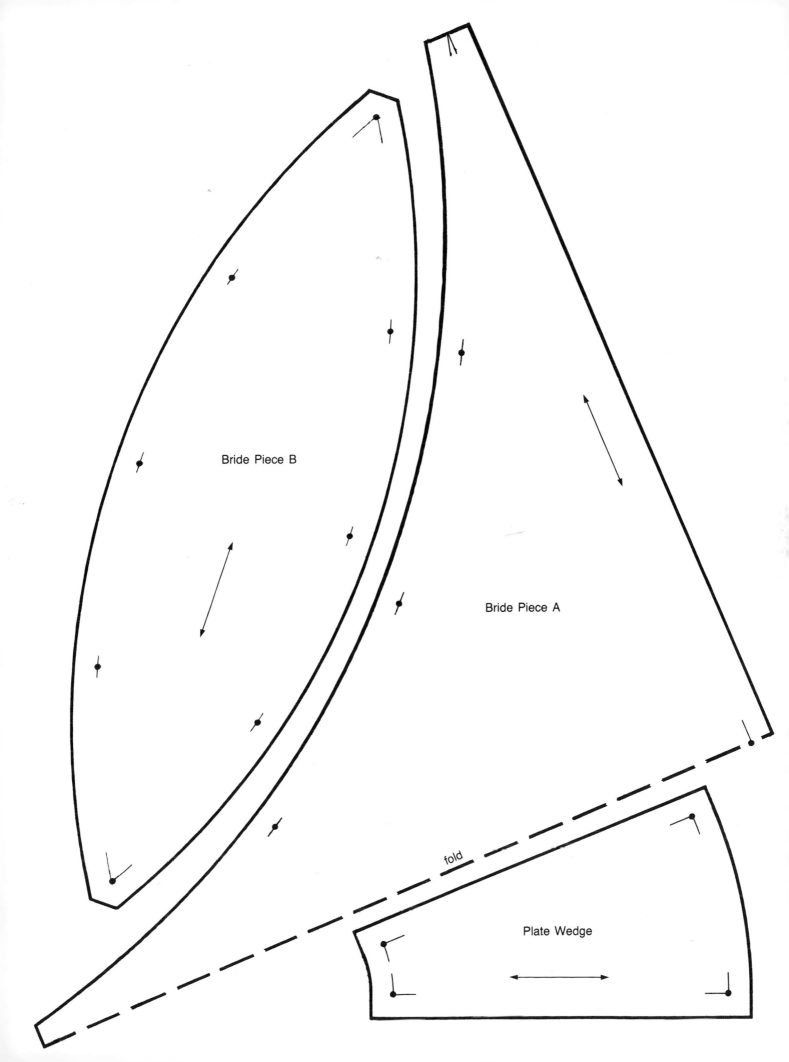

Bride Piece B

Bride Piece A

fold

Plate Wedge

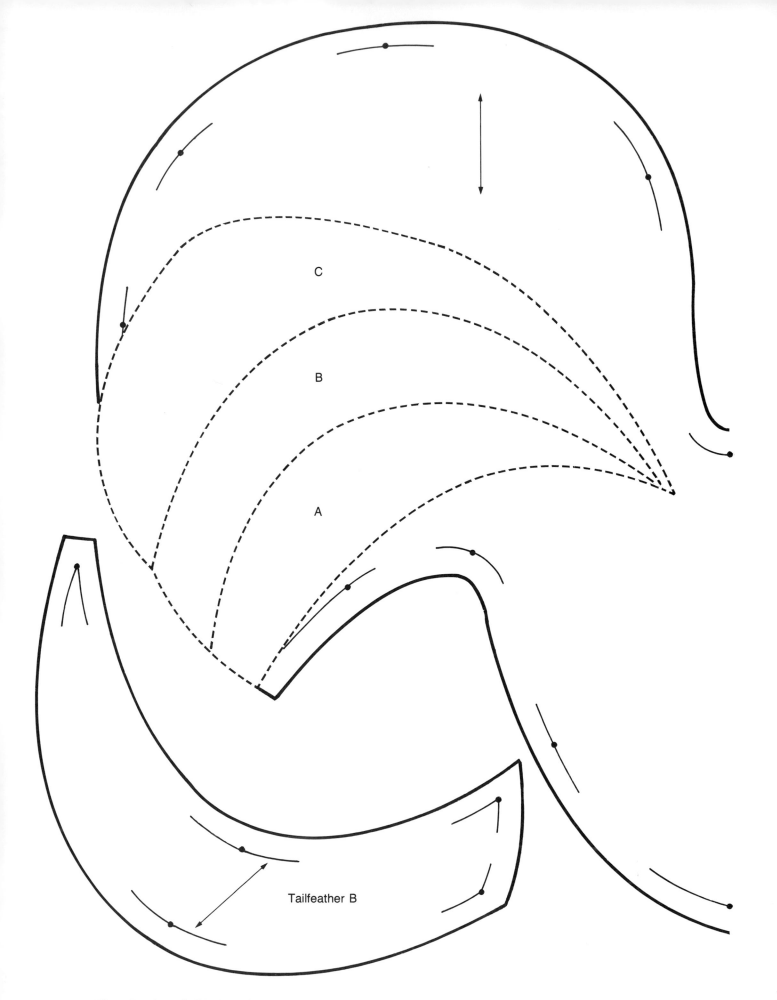

C

B

A

Tailfeather B

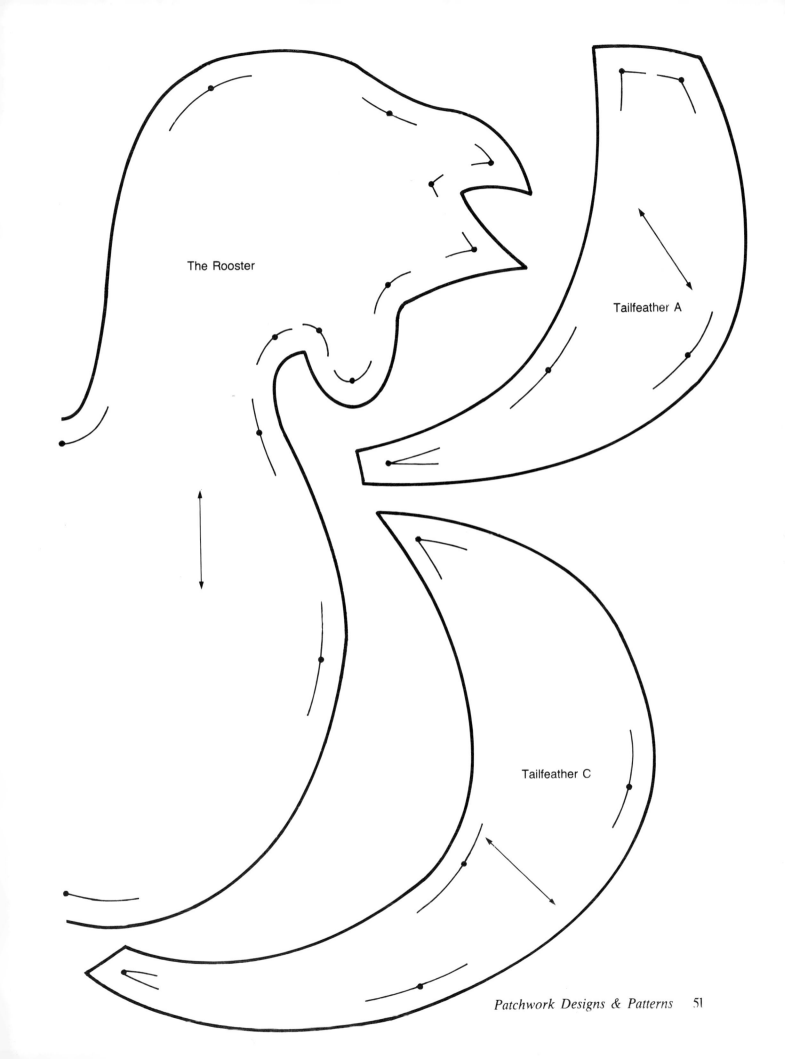

The Rooster

Tailfeather A

Tailfeather C

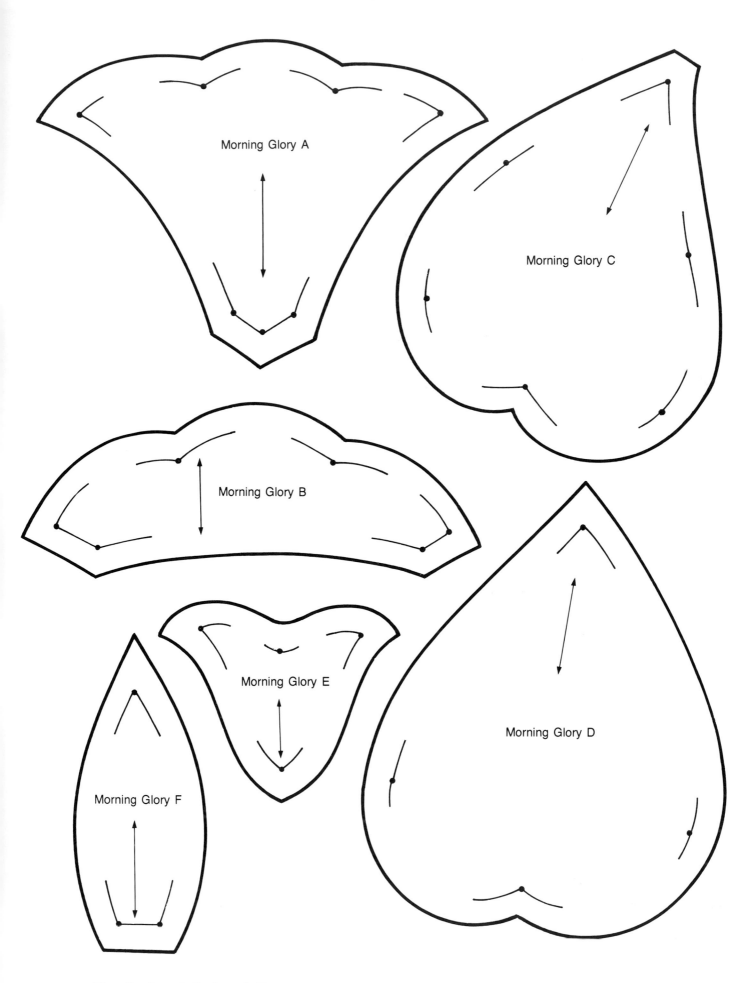

Morning Glory A

Morning Glory C

Morning Glory B

Morning Glory E

Morning Glory F

Morning Glory D

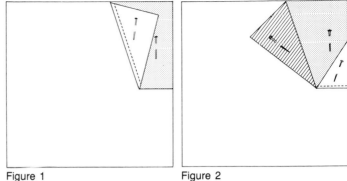

Figure 1   Figure 2

CRAZY PATCH

One traditional design for which no pattern is offered is the crazy patch block. Crazy patch quilts were born of the necessity to use every scrap of material. No specific geometric shapes are used; the overall haphazard appearance of crazy patch is dictated by the shapes of the remnants at hand. This humblest of designs has been used for everything from simple patched coverlets to elegant silk and velvet Victorian throws.

Crazy patch quilting remains popular because of its versatility. Blocks can be made in any shape and can be turned into handbags, vests, quilts—anything that can be sewn. It takes more than a little bit of luck, though, to turn a bag of remnants into a pleasant arrangement. Practice will help you achieve a good balance between light, dark, print, and geometric fabrics, as well as to come up with good combinations of shapes and sizes.

To make a basic crazy patch quilt block, start by cutting a 12½″ square of fabric, such as muslin, to use as a foundation. Then collect your scraps. If this block is to be included in a sampler quilt, why not use the scraps of fabric left over from cutting other blocks? You can combine various weights of fabric with confidence; never rule out an interesting fringe or a buckle from a pair of blue jeans. The only requirements are that the fabric be clean, strong, and ironed flat.

Starting in either the center or the corner of the muslin foundation, pin your first scrap of fabric in place, right side up. Select a second piece and lay it right side down on top of the first, aligning the raw edges of the two pieces along the line where they are to be joined. Pin this second piece and machine stitch the connecting seam with a ¼″ seam allowance, catching both pieces and the foundation. (Figure 1.) Trim the seam allowance, remove the pin, and flip the second piece back over the foundation,

right side now up. Pin it to the foundation and add a third piece in the same "sew and flip" manner. (Figure 2.) Continue to expand the patchwork until the block is covered. Small pieces can be sewn to each other to form rectangles before being sewn to the foundation.

Try to create angles and even curves for variety. Curves, which must be slip stitched in place, are best placed at awkward right angles on the foundation. When you have covered the block, check to be sure that no raw edges remain inside the block; if there are some, simply slip stitch them into place.

Turn the block over, trim it back down to a 12½″ square if necessary, and press it lightly.

Follow tradition and embellish your crazy patch block with embroidery along the internal seam lines. Three basic embroidery stitches to learn are the chain stitch, the buttonhole stitch, and the feather stitch. It is challenging to combine these stitches with one another and to use different colors of thread.

Treat your crazy patch block just as you would any of the other blocks in this book. Quilt it to batting and backing, following the odd shapes of the crazy patches. Large, empty areas may need cross-hatching or curved lines quilted inside of them. Even the back of your crazy patch block will be crazy quilted.

Any of the traditional block designs in this book can incorporate crazy patch. Simply cut one or more of the pattern pieces for the block from muslin and crazy patch onto this muslin foundation.

A particularly effective way to crazy patch inside many designs is string quilting, where long strips of bias or selvage, scraps of lace, and other "strings" of fabric are crazy patched side by side.

First, Piece the Block Together

You've chosen your design and have selected and prepared your fabric. You know how many of which blocks you'll be using and how you plan to set them together. Now it's time to cut your fabric and piece each block together.

TEMPLATES

Making Your Templates

Templates are your guides in cutting the geometric shapes which, when sewn together, will form your blocks. The template patterns offered in the last chapter are traditional patterns based on a 12″ square block. In each pattern piece, a ¼″ seam allowance has been included.

Precision in drawing your templates and transferring them to cloth is essential. If the templates have a firm, hard edge this step will be easier. The geometric shapes may be transferred from this book to templates in two ways. First, using a pencil and ruler, trace the exact lines onto tracing paper. Glue the tracing paper onto thin poster board or cardboard with rubber cement and let dry overnight. Smooth clear Contact® paper onto the top side of each piece of cardboard to protect the patterns. Cut out each figure with paper scissors.

If you prefer, you can trace the shapes onto frosted acetate, using a ruler and permanent pen, and then cut them out with paper scissors. This leaves a perfect, long-lasting template.*

You may also want to glue sandpaper to the backs of your templates. This will keep them from sliding on the fabric. Sandpaper can get expensive, but will make handling the templates much easier. Whichever method of making templates you use, be sure to record on each template all the information you will need about it, such as the grain line and the code lettering.

Quilts have been passed down from generation to generation. But the patterns for them have not fared as well; they probably wore out from constant use. Now, using plastic and cardboard templates, you can pass on your patterns as well as your quilts.

Transferring Templates to Cloth

After your templates are prepared, you are ready to transfer the patterns onto cloth. The ideal method calls for cutting one piece at a time, but, "oh, an eternity." Fudging a bit, but not sacrificing perfection, calls for doubling the material. The fabric may be folded with either wrong or right sides out.

Excluding the selvage, carefully align templates according to the grain line. Hold the template firmly against the fabric and trace around it with a pencil, fabric marker, tailor's chalk, or with a thin sliver of worn soap. (Never use a ball-point pen or permanent marker; they could run onto the fabric.) When possible, borrow one straight edge from a previously marked pattern piece to save fabric. (Figure 1.) Catch

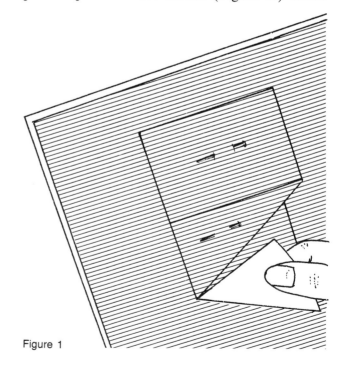

Figure 1

* If you cannot find a good material for templates in your area, write: Plastic, P.O. Box 96, Flat Rock, NC 28731

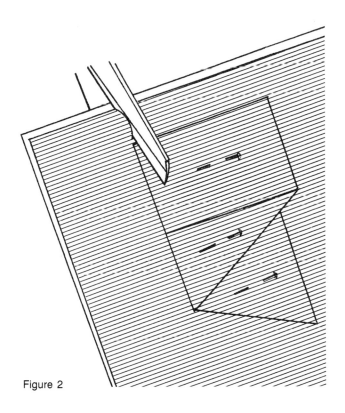

Figure 2

the double layers of fabric with one straight pin to hold the fabric in place as you remove the templates. Then cut the shape with cloth scissors. Do not use pinking shears. (Figure 2.)

MACHINE PIECING

Do you have a good rapport with your sewing machine? Are you on the same wavelength? Read the instructions to your sewing machine. Each machine has its own idiosyncrasies; get to know them. Then, if your machine is in good working order, piecing will be a joy.

If you use a portable machine on a kitchen table, be sure it is at a convenient height for sewing. You may want to try sitting on a couple of catalogues or pillows so that you are looking down on the needle as the fabric glides through the machine. If you sew with an all-purpose foot, check the distance from the needle to the outside edge of the foot; you may find that it is ¼″, making it a good guide for seam allowance. If not, masking tape can be placed on the throat plate ¼″ from the needle, as can a magnetic attachment available at sewing notions counters. The ability to sew a true ¼″ seam allowance comes with practice; do not expect perfection at

first. Just as in any new learning experience, trial and error is involved, so be patient. Some materials sew together better than others. Be conscious of the diagonal bias lines of triangles and avoid stretching them when sewing.

Use a compatible, dual duty thread on the machine. A neutral shade such as beige or gray works well with many blocks. Do not use quilting thread on the machine; save it for your handwork. Take the time to load several bobbins and you will always be ready when one bobbin runs out.

Keep the block design chosen from the last chapter, showing the completed block, near the machine to guide you as you sew the block together. Study the pattern code beneath each block design and find your smallest pieces; these will be sewn together first. Is your block a four patch, nine patch, or one that depends on a center assembly such as Log Cabin or Formal Garden? Know how each block is constructed and broken down into sections. The broken lines along the outside of each design help with the assembly. Be sure to consult the next section, Special Tips at the Sewing Machine, for hints on constructing many of the blocks.

If you are in the habit of sewing over pins at a right angle, be my guest. I do pin sets together in the middle to anchor them and also place pins at intersections, but I do not sew over them. Backstitching is unnecessary—all seams will be crossed and therefore secured.

Never open the seams in piecework. This would weaken the piecework and make it more vulnerable. When possible, crease and press seams toward the darker fabric patch; this keeps the seam allowance from showing through a lighter piece. Taking the time to think ahead when putting a block together will help in achieving a well-balanced block.

SPECIAL TIPS AT THE SEWING MACHINE

Quickie Piece Method

Whenever two identical right-angled triangles are to be sewn together several times in a block, you can use a shortcut method of machine piecing. This Quickie Piece Method will save a great deal of time, especially when you are repeating the same block many times in a quilt.

The Quickie Piece Method can be used whenever two right-angled triangles are to be joined along their long sides to form a square. Simply lay out the two contrasting fabrics you are using, right sides together. Count the number of squares made up of two triangles that are included in your block; trace the triangle template that number of times onto the wrong side of the fabric as shown. (Figure 1.)

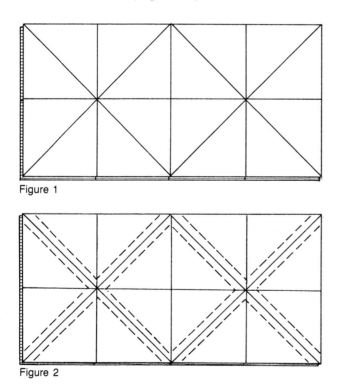

Figure 1

Figure 2

Using a ruler, carefully draw another line ¼" from each diagonal line, on both sides of the diagonal line. (Figure 2.) This new set of lines

represents your sewing line. Machine stitch along it continuously.

After machine stitching, cut the fabric along the lines originally drawn. (Figure 3.) Your triangles are sewn into squares before they are even cut!

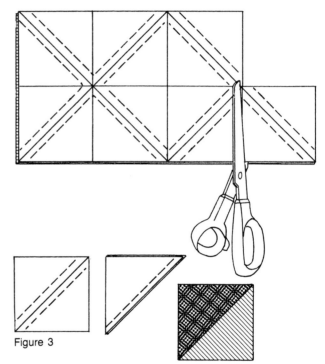

Figure 3

With one minor difference, this same method can be used when two right-angled triangles are to be joined to form a larger triangle. In this case, mark your sewing line on both sides of only one continuous diagonal line. (Figure 4.)

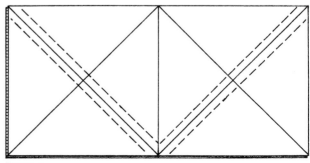

Figure 4

Quickie Strip Method

Strip patchwork is the technique of sewing several long strips of contrasting fabrics together to form a striped band. The striped band is then cut into segments that can be rearranged into new patterns. This method of piecing fabric together is a real time-saver whenever several squares or rectangles of the same width are to be joined in the same color sequence.

A good example of when to use the Quickie Strip Method is in the Corner Nine Patch design. Four of its patches are made up of three rectangles joined in the same dark-light-dark sequence. Rather than cutting each of these rectangles separately, cut three strips of fabric, two dark and one light; because the block is repeated four times, each strip should be four times the width of the rectangles. Machine stitch the three strips together into a band (Figure 5); then cut the band into four equal pieces (Figure 6). The corner patches of the Corner Nine Patch pattern can be assembled in a similar manner, cutting striped bands the width of the small squares.

Piecing Four Patch Blocks

The basic four patch patterns are each made up of four 6″ blocks that are constructed in a similar manner and are then stitched together to make a 12″ block.

You'll be tempted to put each of the four small blocks together independently, but wait! You'll save time and have a better alignment if you take an assembly line approach. If each of these quarter sections has a triangle connected to a trapezoid, for instance, make those four connections in a continuous manner. Put your four sets of triangles and trapezoids together by laying them out, right sides touching, aligning their raw edges, and then pinning. Slide the first set through the machine; sew on air for a moment; lift the presser foot and ease another set through. (Figure 1.) When all four seams are made, cut stitching between sets. Then add the other pieces needed to make each quarter section. Counting the seam allowance, each quarter section should be the size of Square A.

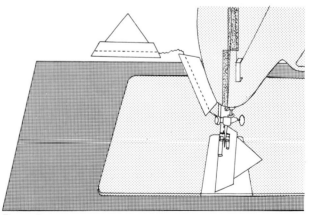
Figure 1

Connect quarter sections according to the block design (pages 12-29). An ⅛″ "off-ness" at the seam can be fudged, but anything smaller or larger than ¼″ means back to the cutting board. If you cut your pieces too large or take too small a seam allowance your piecework will grow and you'll lose the points on stars. It is natural at first to take too large a seam allowance; if

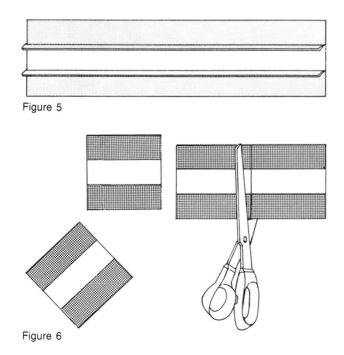
Figure 5

Figure 6

you've done that, or have cut your pieces too small, your quarter section will shrink.

There are exceptions to the quarter section assembly. One is Road to Oklahoma, where it is best to work in rectangles due to the trapezoids. The following are special tips for assembling the four-patch patterns in this book.

 Rail Fence—Lay out eight sets of two F rectangles and sew them in the continuous piecing method described above. Match each set of two to another set and sew, resulting in four squares made up of four rectangles each. Press seams in an outward direction and check quarter section size; with ¼" seam allowance all around, it should now measure 6½". Sew two quarter sections together; repeat with second set. Now pin the two half sections together, staggering seams in the center, and sew.

 King's X—Lay out four sets of two A trapezoids and sew them together in the continuous piecing method described above. Sew H triangles to each of the eight short sides, letting the same amount of "dog ear" extend from the triangles. Consult block diagram and set the quarter sections in the proper arrangement; sew and press all seams in a clockwise direction so that they will automatically stagger.

Kansas Trouble—Lay out sixteen sets of two J triangles and sew together to form squares; then sew eight sets of two squares together to form rectangles. Add a dark J triangle to the end of each rectangle; the shape that results will be referred to as a "star section." Add a C square to the end of four of the star sections. Attach the remaining four star sections to Triangle H; then add to Triangle H the four star sections to which squares were

attached. You will have four pieced triangles. Each is now attached to a Triangle E to form quarter sections.

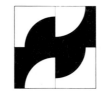 **Drunkard's Path**—Place a pin at the midpoint of each curve; align pins as pieces are joined. If pins are not aligning at midpoint, ease fabric until the end of the seam. The bottom fabric shifts to the left and the top comes to meet the raw edge. Clip seams to press them outward; notch them to press in.

 Coffee Cup—Sew together two light B squares. Appliqué handle to the rectangle formed. Piece together quarter sections according to the block design and assemble as a four patch.

 Cube Accent—For each quarter section, form trapezoids by sewing C triangles to C parallelograms (four per quarter section). Sew the trapezoids to the center B square by pivoting with the needle in the material; or by sewing sides only up to the ¼" seam allowance, leaving angled seams to be sewn in a separate step.

 Bow Tie—Sew the short side of one A pentagon to the side of the center G square; sew the short side of another pentagon to the opposite side of the square. Pivot the remaining two pentagons into place at the seam intersection. The needle must be in the seam to hold this turn in place. Pivot at the 135 degree angle; it will not work at right angles.

King's X design and a variation of it made by rearranging its quarter sections.

Above: *Saw Tooth Star design with mitered borders and bias edging.*
Above right: *Sampler quilt with scalloped edge cut out of mitered borders on the perimeter of the quilt.*
Right: *Sampler quilt with inside mitered borders and ruffled edges.*
Opposite: *Attic Windows design with two outside borders, one solid and one pieced.*

Piecing Log Cabin Blocks

The basic Log Cabin block and its variations rely on the addition of contrasting rectangles to a central square. Cut all strips the same width as indicated by the pattern, but in varying lengths. Machine stitch the shortest strip to the central square, trim ends even with the square, and crease the seam to the outside. Then add the other strips one at a time in a continuous circle. (An inch line can be drawn from a previous row to keep you on target.) Keep adding until there are five strips on all four sides of the center square.

Log Cabin—To form each circle of strips, sew two light strips, then two dark strips. You may use two different light fabrics as long as both contrast to the dark fabric.

Log Cabin Variation #1—Sew the same fabric on all four sides for each circular row, alternating fabrics with each row. This pattern is sometimes called Around the World.

Log Cabin Variation #2—Alternate fabrics with each strip added. The resulting Courthouse Steps pattern will have opposite sides of the same fabric.

Log Cabin Four Patch—Make quarter sections by adding two rows of contrasting fabric to each of the center squares. Assemble the four sections to form one block.

Grandmother's Fan design with inside mitered borders and ruffled edging.

Piecing Nine Patch Blocks

The nine patch blocks, beginning with Basic Nine Patch and ending with Another Star (pages 21-24), are sewn in the assembly line manner described for four-patch blocks (page 57). Each patch should be the size of the E square. Sew three sets of two patches together in a continuous manner; clip apart. Then add one patch to each set. Staggering seams, sew together these three rows of three squares to complete the block.

Piecing Combination Blocks

Moon Over the Mountain and Four Seasons—Sew the three moon sections to the three sky sections, forming three triangles; sew two sets of two triangles forming two large triangles. Be sure to stagger moon-to-sky seams so that they alternate and will connect perfectly. (Figure 1.)

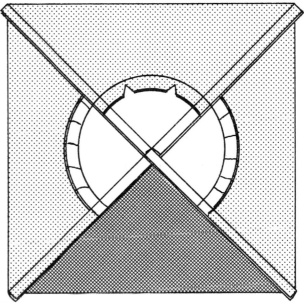

Figure 1

Grandmother's Fan and Dresden Plate—Sew small wedges in twos first, then in fours, etc. Attach quarter circle as in Drunkard's Path instructions (page 58); attach rickrack or lace to the raw edge which can then be turned under, hiding raw edge and revealing half of the rickrack or lace. Place the fan or plate on a 12½"-square piece of foundation material and slip stitch in the "ditch" to secure. Hand baste the opening of Dresden Plate under ¼" so that the contrasting circle can be slipped underneath and slip stitched in place.

Monkey Wrench—Sew together the center four patch; then add the four H triangles to the sides of the square. Make sure that the same amount of "dog ear" extends from each side. Repeat this procedure with the two remaining sets of triangles.

Hexagon Flowerette—Connect the pieces of each vertical row by machine. You will have two rows of three pieces and two rows of four pieces; the center row will consist of five pieces. Now pivot one row into the next. (Figure 2.) Baste under ¼" seam allowance and appliqué the flowerette to a 12½" foundation.

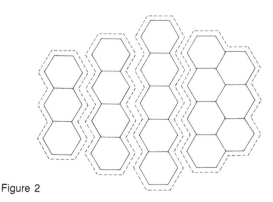

Figure 2

Spider Web—Sew a C trapezoid to each of the P triangles. Sew these larger triangles together in sections of four. Connect to form an octagon; the seam will be at an angle. Attach the corner Q triangles to square off the block.

Cross & Crown—Assemble the four corner patches; attach one to each side of an I rectangle. Form the center row and sew it to the two larger rectangles.

Pieced Little Dutch Boy—Sew J triangle to D pentagon and add C pentagon to form body. Appliqué an arm to each R triangle before sewing these to the body. Appliqué both feet to one G triangle and then sew the three G triangles into place. Add E triangles.

Pieced Little Dutch Girl—Sew C triangle to E pentagon; attach D trapezoid. Add an R traingle to each side. Appliqué the foot to one G triangle and then add the three G triangles. Add E triangles. Appliqué the arm; if a hand is desired, fold a 1" square in half, find the midpoint of the side opposite the fold, and crease the folded corners toward it, forming a triangle. Consider adding lace to the front of the hat.

Pressing

Having ready access to an iron as you work is the ideal situation. Thumb creasing is only temporary. Once the block is assembled, steam press it on the back side, directing the seams in the same direction they have been sewn. Turn over the block and press on the top side to eliminate any creases. Trim any "dog ears" and your block will be ready for border attachment or block-to-block assembly.

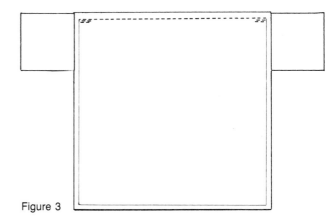

Figure 3

Marking the Seam Allowance

The next step is mandatory! Cut a perfect 12″ square from plastic or poster board. Center this on the back side of your block and trace around it, marking a ¼″ seam allowance on all four sides. Do not cut this off; it is a guide to follow when attaching borders or sewing blocks to one another. Even when the same fabrics and the same patterns are used, blocks will vary in size. In a sampler quilt, block sizes may be quite different, so don't skip this important step.

BORDERS

If the design for your quilt calls for borders, you will find that a neat, mitered border frames each block beautifully. Varying the colors and sizes of the borders from block to block can also help you achieve a wide variety of effects, but one thing remains constant: the border for any given block must be the same width on all four sides.

The designs in this book are based on 12″-square blocks with 3″-wide borders, resulting in 18″-square finished blocks. In order to achieve this, you will need to cut four 3½″ x 19″ pieces of fabric for the borders for one block. Always cut the long side of a border along the lengthwise grain of fabric. If you want a smaller or larger border, follow this formula:

Decide on the border width (let's say 4″) and add to it ½″ for two ¼″ seam allowances (4½″); this figure is your cutting width.

To calculate cutting length, take the width of your basic block (12½″) and subtract ½″ for two seam allowances (12″); add to that figure twice the cutting width of the borders (12″ + 4½″ + 4½″ = 21″).

Mitering Corners

Follow these steps carefully for a perfect mitered corner:

Step 1: Place one border strip on the edge of the block, right sides together, so that equal amounts extend from each side. (Figure 3.)

Step 2: With the block wrong side up, machine stitch the border with a ¼″ seam allowance, following the straight line previously drawn. Do not start sewing at the raw edge, but ¼″ inside, on the corner line already drawn. Fold the border out so that it extends from the block. Now add the other three borders, each time sewing up close to the right angle. Backstitch to secure corners. Note the right angle formed outside each corner of the block. There will be a 3½″ extension on each end.

Step 3: Let borders extend outward with overlapping. Each outside edge becomes a guide to trim off the excess of the other borders. There is a perfect right angle overlap at each corner. (Figure 4.)

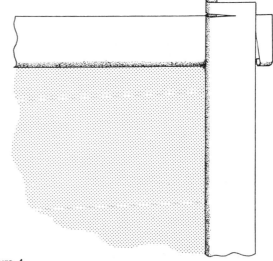

Figure 4

Step 4: Fold the right sides together of adjacent borders, forming a triangle at the corners, and

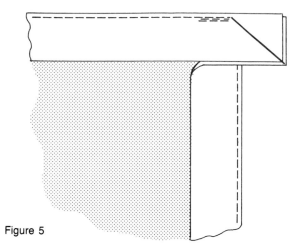

Figure 5

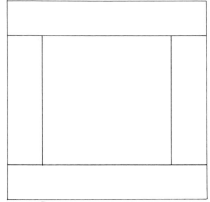

Figure 6

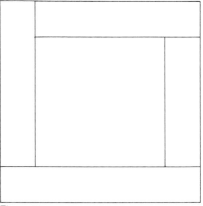

Figure 7

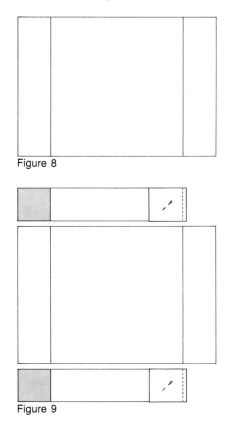

Figure 8

Figure 9

draw a straight line from inside the backstitching point to the outside corner on the border material. Machine sew along this line, backstitching at the inside and sewing outward to the tip. (Figure 5.) Trim a ¼″ seam allowance and press seams between block and border in the same direction, either towards the block (if you want to quilt on the border) or away from the block (if you want to quilt inside the block, close to the border). Press the diagonal, mitered seam in a clockwise direction on each corner.

Strip Addition: An Alternative

If your design calls for borders, but you don't want mitered corners, strips can frame your blocks in a number of ways.

The first method calls for two strips cut the width of your choice and the length of the block. These are sewn to opposite sides of the block. To the remaining sides, add strips cut long enough to include the width of the first strips sewn. (Figure 6.)

A similar effect can be achieved by adding strips sewn in the Log Cabin fashion, starting on one side and adding strips in a circular fashion. (Figure 7.)

Adding square accents to corners is another effective border treatment. Add strips to two opposite sides first. (Figure 8.) Then sew corners to one end of each of the remaining two strips. Pin corners and find the exact placement of the opposite square before sewing in place. (Figure 9.) Stagger seams for the strongest connection.

Next, Quilt Each Block

MARKING THE QUILTING PATTERN

Whether your finished quilt will be made up of individual blocks with borders or of groups of blocks sewn together without borders, the next step in lap quilting is transferring the stencil designs to your blocks. These designs become your path to follow in making your quilting stitches. The way they are placed on the fabric is very important; they must be easy to follow for quilting, yet simple to remove once the quilting is completed.

The secret to lap quilting is keeping at least ½" to 1" around each side of a block unquilted. A quilting design such as cross-hatching, which is handsome for pillows and place mats, does not work well on the borders of lap quilting blocks that will eventually be connected; the lines extend out to the raw edges, preventing assembly of the blocks.

Before transferring stencils to fabric, make sure each block has been well pressed and will lie flat. Choose a marking implement—a fabric pen or pencil, a sliver of soap, or tailor's chalk—and test it to be sure it can be easily removed from the fabric. Once you've chosen the quilting pattern you want, there are several methods of transferring it to the fabric.

Try placing light colored fabric directly on top of the dark-lined patterns in this book (pages 68-76). If you can see the pattern through the fabric, simply trace the pattern directly onto the fabric with any removeable marking device.

Unless your fabric is very light in color, though, you will need to trace the pattern onto paper with a heavy marker, place the paper under the fabric, and find a way to illuminate the paper and fabric from behind. A sunny window works well, as does a glass-topped table with a light below it. Or you can improvise a light box from a cardboard box by putting a hole in the bottom or side for a light and taping a piece of glass to the top.

You can also make cardboard or plastic templates. (See page 54.) Position the templates on the fabric and trace around the designs, using either a continuous line or dots.

If you prefer, cut the stencil shape out of Contact® paper. The shape will adhere to the fabric while you're quilting around it; then simply remove it and stick it to the next area to be quilted. This method eliminates the use of pen or pencil parks. Masking tape in various widths makes a handy guide for quilting straight lines.

DESIGNS FOR STENCILS

The stencils on the following pages will give you some ideas for quilting designs for borders as well as for inside your blocks. There is no limit to the designs you can create on your own.

Although some ideas are presented here for quilting inside your blocks, you may find that simple outline quilting best accentuates your chosen pattern. Outline quilting is usually done ⅛" to ¼" from the seam line and follows the shapes of the pattern pieces in the block.

Don't overlook the possibilities that lie in the shapes of everyday items around your house. Cookie cutters, cups and saucers, and even children's toys can be your instant templates.

(Half of design.)

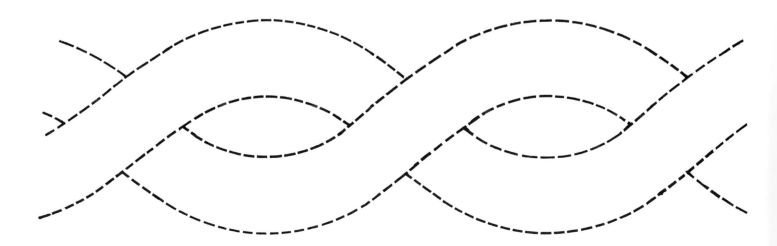

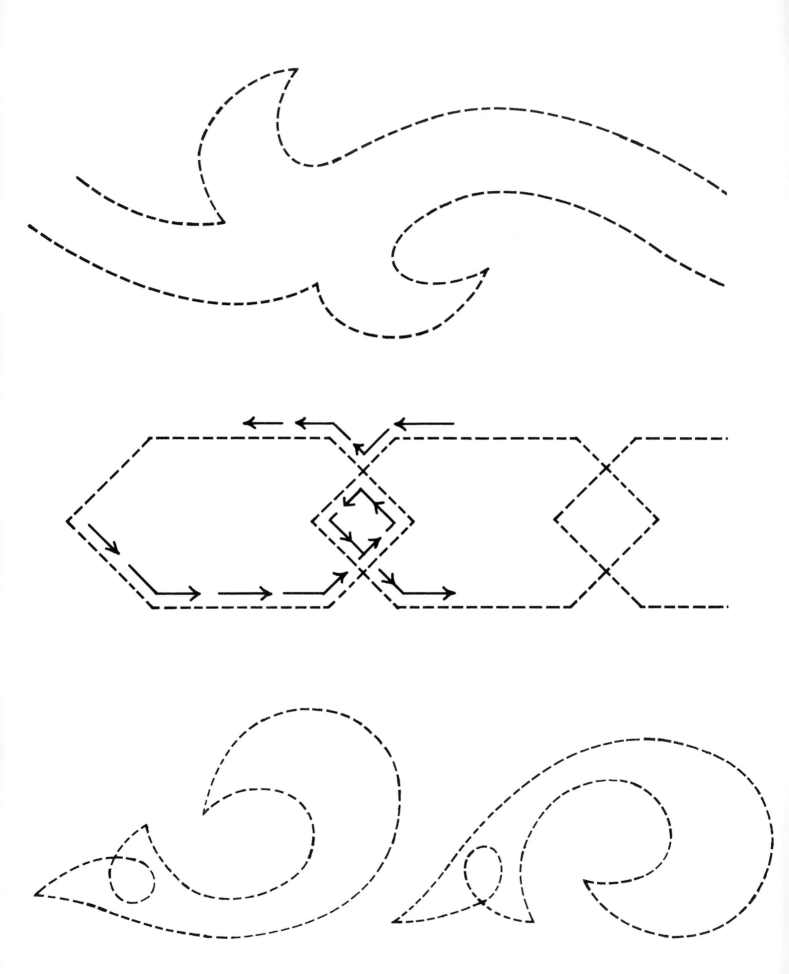

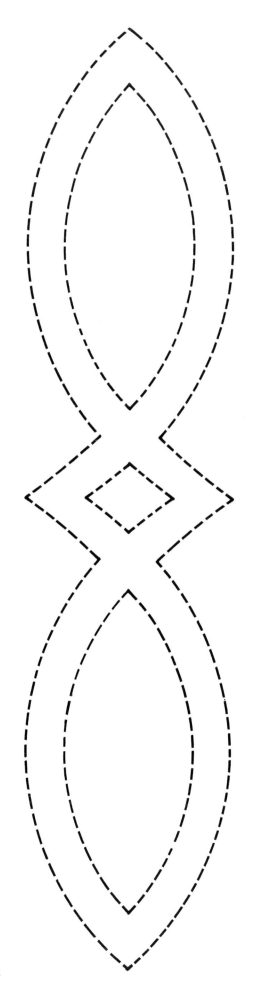

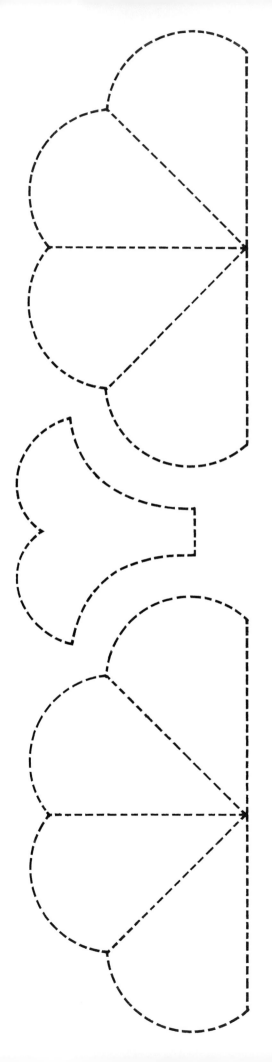

(Quarter of design.)

center

(Half of design.)

THE THREE B'S—BATTING, BACKING & BASTING

The stencil-marked blocks are your pattern for cutting the batting and backing. Whether you have added a border to a 12″ block (Method A) or have sewn four blocks together without borders (Method B), your dimensions should already include outside seam allowances, so there is no need to cut a larger backing. If you plan to create a design on the back of the quilt by alternating backing fabrics, remember that as you cut out your backing.

After cutting out the backing and batting, align them with the block and pin the three layers together. Baste layers together around the outside, with an X through the middle, and at right angles. (Figure 1.) Use a contrasting thread for basting that can be seen easily for removal.

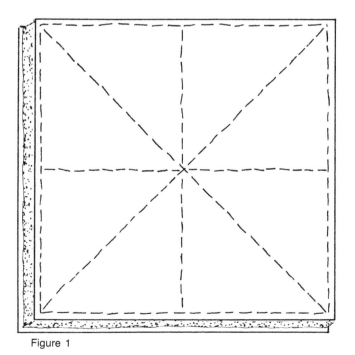

Figure 1

QUILTING GUIDELINES

Connecting these three layers with tiny quilting stitches is what quilting is all about. The following guidelines are important to remember as you quilt your blocks.

Whether or not you use a frame, it is important to quilt in the center of each block first. Then proceed to the outside edges. Remember to stop quilting ½″ to 1″ short of the outside edge of your block so that you can connect the blocks later. Try to put approximately the same amount of quilting in each block; your stitches will take up some of the fabric, but you want the blocks to be the same size. This is especially important in sampler quilts.

Polyester batting gives you great freedom; large areas can be left unquilted, since the batting will not separate and get lumpy with washing like old-fashioned cotton batting.

The fewer the knots, the more durable the quilt, so eliminate as many knots as you can. When possible, sneak the needle through the batting to the next area to be quilted rather than ending off with a knot. A thread that is cut too long and pulled through the layers repeatedly will wear and fray. The use of beeswax is optional; quilting thread comes with a coating.

Take small, consistently uneven stitches (a sewing machine would make consistently even stitches), about six to ten stitches per inch. Let your off hand gently hold the material and check to see that the needle point has come through all three layers. Also use your off hand to be sure there is no overlapping of backing material. If overlapping occurs, stop, take the offending quilting stitches out, and start again. Try to take up the same amount of material on the top and the backing.

If you prefer to use a round hoop or square frame, the rocking method of quilting will be best for you. Negotiate the needle through the layers by controlling the eye of the needle with your thimble. Your thumb remains free or rests

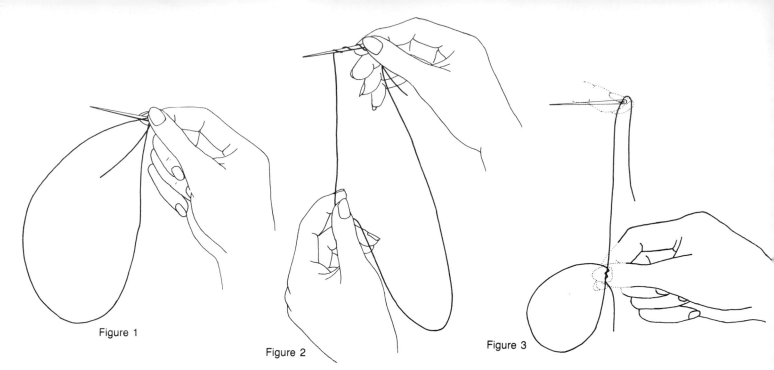

Figure 1

Figure 2

Figure 3

on the quilt top. With a frame, the tension of the material is maintained by adjusting the screw on the side.

Outline quilting within the pieced design beautifully accentuates the geometric piecing. Quite often it is only necessary to quilt on one side of a seamline inside the block. Try to choose the side that does not have the seam allowance, and you'll avoid unnecessary bulk. Quilting lines should run ⅛″ to ¼″ from the seamline; remember that the seamline is your guide, and will help you to quilt in a straight line. The further you get from that line, the easier it will be for your line of stitches to become crooked. I do not recommend quilting in the "ditch," exactly on the connecting seamline; any quilting stitches there are obscure. If you like the look of quilting ¼″ from the seamline, try placing ¼″-wide masking tape along the seam and quilting along the opposite edge of the tape. Then remove the tape and place it on the next area to be quilted. Remember that special shapes cut from masking tape or Contact® paper should not be left on the fabric for long periods of time or they may become difficult to remove.

There are two approaches to taking your quilting stitches. The first is to cut a 30″ length of quilting thread and pull it halfway into the block, leaving the other half dangling freely. Now start quilting with a running stitch, taking two or three stitches at a time; or with a rocking stitch, using a short needle and a thimble.

Quilt right angle lines first, and then go on to the diagonal lines where the fabric has more give. When you reach the end of the thread, end off by looping the thread into a knot and taking a half-backstitch into the batting; do not go through to the backing. Come up about an inch away and tug at the thread until the knot pops through the fabric into the batting. Clip the thread; the floater thread will be hidden inside the batting.

Rethread the needle with the length of thread left dangling before your first stitch and quilt in the opposite direction. End off.

A second approach commonly used calls for a shorter thread and a small, foolproof knot, which can be pulled through the fabric to hide in the batting.

To make a foolproof knot, thread the needle with 12″ to 18″ of quilting thread. Hold the eye of the needle with your right thumb and forefinger. Draw the longer length of thread into a circle, aiming at the tip of the needle, until you can grasp its end, with the needle eye, in your right hand. (Figure 1.) Wrap the thread around the needle two or three times with your left hand. Slide this coil of thread down the needle until you can hold it, along with the eye and the thread end, in your right hand. (Figure 2.) Holding the end of the needle with your left hand, slide the coil down the thread until it tightens. (Figure 3.) Trim any tail off the end. You'll have a perfect knot every time.

Sails in the Sunset design with outside borders and bias edging.

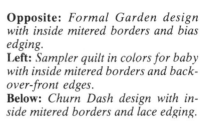

Opposite: *Formal Garden design with inside mitered borders and bias edging.*
Left: *Sampler quilt in colors for baby with inside mitered borders and back-over-front edges.*
Below: *Churn Dash design with inside mitered borders and lace edging.*

Opposite: *Dresden Delight, an oversized adaptation of the Dresden Plate design.*
Right: *Brasstown Star design with optional corner insets.*
Below: *Log Cabin design with saw-toothed edging.*

Left: *White-on-white sampler quilt with inside mitered borders and eyelet edging.*
Below: *Pinwheel design alternated with plain, quilted blocks. An optional outside border was added.*

Churn Dash design with inside mitered borders and contrasting bias edging.

Now, Put Your Quilt Together

All your blocks are quilted and you're no doubt dying to see how they'll look together as a finished quilt. All of your effort, time, and patience are about to be realized; before you know it, your quilt will be assembled, its edges bound, and you'll be able to snuggle up under it on a cool evening.

Before you begin assembling the quilt, remove any fabric marker lines from your blocks with a clean, wet sponge, and pull out any basting threads. Trim all four sides of each block so that the edges of the three layers are aligned.

Set the blocks on the floor or bed and decide on their best arrangement. If you've sketched the overall design for your quilt, you already have the map you need to put your blocks together. If not, you will want to play with your blocks until you achieve a good balance of color and design. If your quilt is a sampler, alternate four-patch and nine-patch blocks.

Once you have all of your blocks laid out, take a few steps back, squint your eyes, and be sure that you like what you see. Mark each block with a fabric marker or make a simple diagram on paper so that you will remember the final setting. You'll first assemble the horizontal rows and then attach the rows to each other. This process is the same for Method A (bordered) or Method B (four block) arrangements.

Freehand string quilt made with one pattern piece, Triangle E, and assembled in four-patch blocks.

BLOCK-TO-BLOCK ASSEMBLY

In block-to-block assembly, the blocks are first assembled in horizontal rows. The tops of the blocks are machine sewn to one another, leaving the backing free to be hand sewn in a flat, lapped seam.

Join the Tops
Step 1: Lay the first two blocks side by side on a flat surface, backing side up. Roll back the backing and the batting on the sides that are to be joined and pin them to the backing, revealing the wrong side of the tops of both blocks.

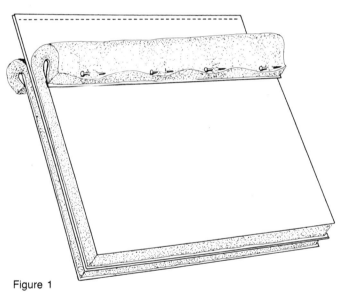

Figure 1

Step 2: Place the two blocks right sides together and align their corners and center sections with pins. (If the corners are mitered, note how the seams stagger automatically because you pressed the seams in one direction.) Ease any excess material between these three pins.
Step 3: Baste the seam; then machine sew a ¼" seam allowance, backstitching at each end. (Figure 1.) If there is extra fullness at the corners of the borders, you may need to sew in a bit more than ¼" at the ends.

If your batting is thin enough, you may want to include the batting from one block in the seam each time two blocks are joined. (Figure 2.) This helps to stabilize the batting within the block assembly, but is by no means essential. Always sew with the batting side down. The

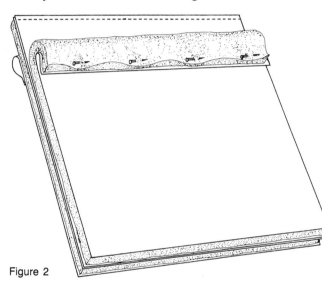

Figure 2

batting will sew easily if it rests on the feed dogs of the machine; do not let it come in contact with the needle. If you are including a layer of batting in the seam, take the batting from the block left of the seam at each connection on the first row; on the second row, switch to taking the batting from the block right of the seam. This will simplify row-to-row connection.

Continue attaching blocks until you have formed a complete horizontal row.

Connect the Backing

Step 1: Lay your row of blocks, backing side up, on a flat surface. Keeping the seams you sewed on the block tops closed, crease each seam in a given horizontal row in the same direction; alternate the direction of the crease from row to row. Unpin the batting and the backing. If the batting is thick, some of it will need to be trimmed from one side so that the two pieces of batting abut. Thinner batting can be permitted

to overlap. You may want to loosely baste at the point where the two pieces of batting meet or overlap, but it is not necessary.

Step 2: Let one side of the backing rest flat on top of the front seam and batting. Turn the other side under ¼" and let it lie on top of the flat piece of backing. Pin the fold in place, placing pins in the center and at both ends of the blocks. Slip stitch this lapped seam closed with a coordinating color of quilting thread, taking care not to go through to the top of the block. (Figure 3.)

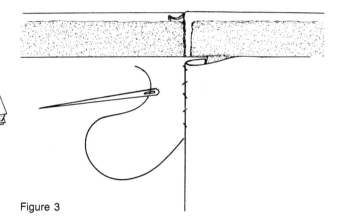

Figure 3

Step 3: If keeping your quilting stitches away from the edges of your blocks prevented you from putting in all the quilting you wanted, you can quilt close to the edges after the blocks are assembled with the aid of a quilting hoop. Or, you can quilt along the edges before the folded lap of backing is stitched into place. This second method is particularly useful when working with mitered corners.

ROW-TO-ROW ASSEMBLY

Assembling the horizontal rows of quilt blocks will finish your quilt except for its outside edges. Consult your diagrams for the correct order in which the rows are to be connected.

Row-to-row assembly can be done in three ways. The method you choose depends on your batting thickness and on how the outside edges of the quilt are to be treated.

Method 1: This method works best when using thick batting or when a ruffle, border, or extra edging is to be added later.

Place two rows to be joined, backing side up, on a flat surface. Roll back and pin the batting and backing of the edges to be connected; then lay the rows top sides together. Pin the tops together at each point that block-to-block seams intersect and ease the fabric between the pins. Baste well along the seam line and then machine stitch a ¼″ seam allowance, back-stitching at each end. (Figure 1.) Crease each row's seam in the same direction. Permit batting to fall and trim one side so that the two pieces of batting will abut. Let one piece of backing lie flat on top of the batting. Turn the other piece of backing under ¼″ and slip stitch it to the flat piece of backing with quilting thread, taking care not to go through to the top of the quilt. (Figure 2.)

Method 2: This method works best when using medium-weight batting and bias edging. Follow the instructions for Method 1, but include the batting from one side in the process of sewing the tops together. (Figure 3.) Be sure to place the batting side down over the feed dogs.

Method 3: This is the simplest of all methods and is suitable when using lightweight batting and bias edging. Place rows top sides together and fold back only the backing from one row. Baste the other five layers together and machine sew with a ¼″ seam allowance. (Figure 4.) Fold the loose piece of backing under ¼″ and slip stitch onto the secured piece of backing.

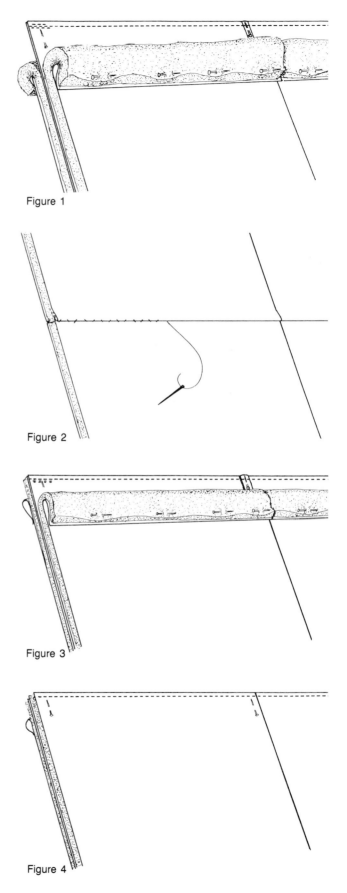

Figure 1

Figure 2

Figure 3

Figure 4

OUTSIDE EDGES

Your moment of glory is close at hand. Your quilted blocks have been assembled into rows and the rows have been sewn together. Now, once you have finished the raw edges of your quilt, it will be ready to show off. There are several options, from the fancy to the functional, for finishing the edges.

Bias Edges

The most popular method for finishing off a quilt is with purchased bias tape or with self-made continuous bias strips. One of the first things to wear out on a quilt is the edging and a double layer of bias at the outside will extend the life of your quilt.

Purchase bias tape that is 2″ wide. Bias strips that you make yourself should be about 2½″ to 3″ wide.

How to make a continuous bias strip.

Start with about 1¼ yards of 45″-wide material. Eliminate the selvage and cut the fabric into a large square. Cut this square on the diagonal, forming two triangles. (Figure 1.)

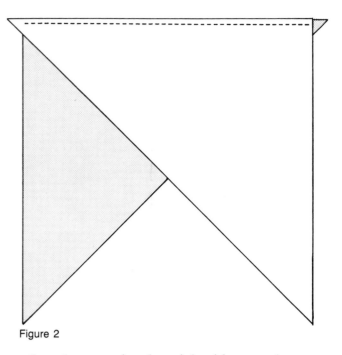

Figure 2

Lay the two triangles, right sides together, so that two perpendicular edges are aligned. (Figure 2.) (Do not join the diagonal edges.) Machine stitch with ¼″ seam allowance. Open the triangles; they will now form a parallelogram. (Figure 3).

Decide how wide you want the bias strip; for the outside of a quilt, 2½″ to 3″ is appropriate. Make a line of this width along the bias edge with a pencil or fabric marker. Cut into the line about 6″. (Figure 3.)

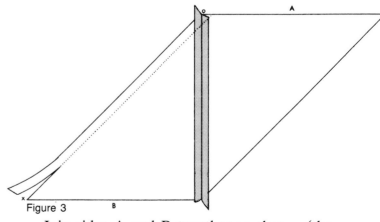

Figure 3

Join sides A and B together so that x (the point just inside the 6″ cut) and o meet with right sides together. Sew a ¼″ seam allowance across this line to form a tube. (Figure 4.) Notice that the cut extends beyond the side of the tube; the other side is similarly uneven. Use the loose bias strip as a pattern to continue

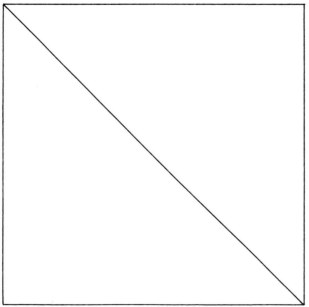

Figure 1

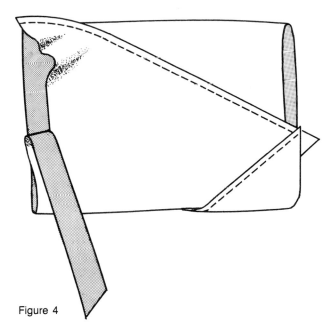

Figure 4

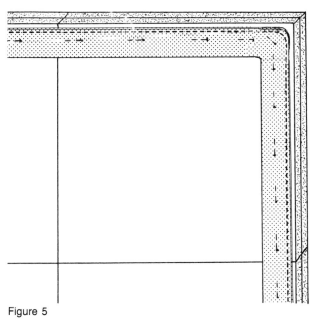

Figure 5

cutting bias around the tube. Keep folding it back, being careful not to cut the material underneath.

How to estimate bias length.

To determine the length of bias you need to make or purchase, first measure the perimeter of your quilt. The following table will help.

METHOD A

Baby quilt size	5 yards
Afghan size	7 yards
Twin size	8 yards
Double size	9 yards
Queen size	11 yards
King size	13 yards

METHOD B

Baby quilt size	5¼ yards
Afghan size	6¾ yards
Twin size	9¼ yards
Double size	10½ yards
King size	13¼ yards

How to attach a continuous bias strip.

Align the raw edges of the continuous bias strip, folding it in half. Place the folded strip on top of the quilt with the strip's fold toward the inside and its raw edges aligning with the raw edges of the quilt. Gently curve the strip around corners. Pin or baste the strip in place. Machine stitch a ¼″ seam allowance. (Figure 5.)

If you are using purchased bias tape, be sure to sew a strong connection where ends of the tape meet. If you are sewing continuous bias strips you've made yourself, start or stop sewing

each strip a few inches from both ends. Where the loose ends meet, let them overlap. Find the point where the bottom layer of side B ends (x) and mark that point on side A. Then find the point where the top layer of side B ends (o) and mark it on side A. (Figure 6.)

Unfold side A and mark points ½″ to the right of x and o. Draw a line between this second set of points and cut along it. (Figure 7.) Once you have cut, you will find you can join the two sides with a perfect ¼″ seam allowance. Fold again and secure to the quilt.

After you have machine sewn the bias to the quilt top, roll the bias over the raw edges and slip stitch it in place just over the machine stitching on the back of the quilt.

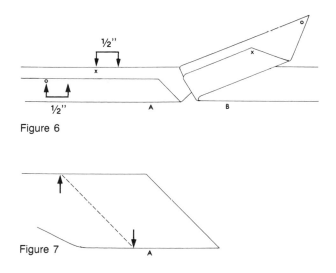

Figure 6

Figure 7

Self-Finished Edges

For a simple, neat edge treatment, trim about ¼″ of batting all around the perimeter of your quilt, turn raw edges of the quilt top and backing towards each other, and stitch. A running stitch is best. The corners may remain square.

Back-Over-Front Edges

Another favorite finishing technique is to cut backings 1″ larger on the outside edge of each perimeter block. Bring the backing around to the front edge, turn its raw edges under ¼″ and secure it with a tight slip stitch.

Ruffles and Such

To attach ruffles, eyelet, cording or pleats to the quilt, machine sew them to the top edge of the quilt with a ¼″ seam allowance, catching the batting but letting the backing remain free. (Figure 8.) Trim away any excess seam allowance; turn raw edges in toward the center; turn backing under ¼″ and slip stitch it over the line of machine stitching.

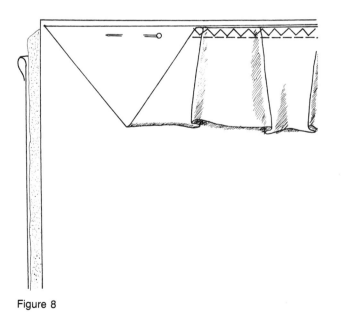

Figure 8

Saw-Toothed and Scalloped Edges

Decorative saw-toothed or scalloped edgings can be made by attaching fabric to the edges in the same manner as a ruffle. To make the saw-toothed edges, fold 5″ squares into triangles once; then refold them into smaller triangles. These can be interlapped for a saw-toothed edging. (Figure 1.) Five triangles will form an 18″-long section. Smaller squares make a very effective edging for a baby quilt.

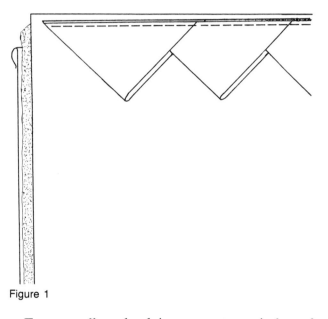

Figure 1

For a scalloped edging, sew two circles of material together. Cut through the diameter, and turn right side out to form two half circles. Sew the half circles side by side to form a lovely scalloped edge.

If you like the look of a scalloped edge, but would prefer to be able to quilt it, it is best to sew a three-layered edging before attaching it to the quilt. In this case, make each side's edging out of pieces of continuous fabric. Make a template and trace the scallop design onto the wrong side of your quilt top fabric with the straight edge on the straight of the grain. Stack this piece of fabric with pieces of batting and backing the same size; stack batting, backing fabric right side up, and then quilt top fabric wrong side up. Baste the three layers together and then machine stitch along the curved edge of the scalloped border, taking an extra horizontal stitch at each "V" before sewing around the next curve. (Figure 2.) Trim all three layers along the straight edge of the scallop and around the now-sewn curves; turn inside out and attach to the raw edges of the quilt.

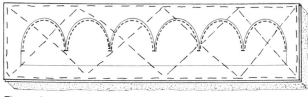

Figure 2

This same method can be used to attach a scalloped border to an already edged quilt. Quilting can be done on the scalloped edge or border after attaching it to the quilt.

Another version of the scalloped edge can be made by actually cutting scallops into the perimeter borders of the blocks that will form the outside edges of the quilt. This method calls for tracing the scallop design on the wrong side of the top of the block before it is quilted. Baste block backing and batting together and put the right sides of the block and backing together so that machine stitching the three layers is possible, following the curved scallop. Here again, take one horizontal stitch at the "V" between curves to give a flat, easy turn. Trim away excess material; turn inside out, and baste. Quilt close to the perimeter edge.

Borders

If your quilt isn't large enough after your edging has been applied, or if you feel that you need to frame it, it is never too late to sew on a border. Using continuous pieces of fabric, cut strips for the front, back, and batting the same size. Stack the fabric as follows, laying fabric with its raw edges aligned with the edge of the

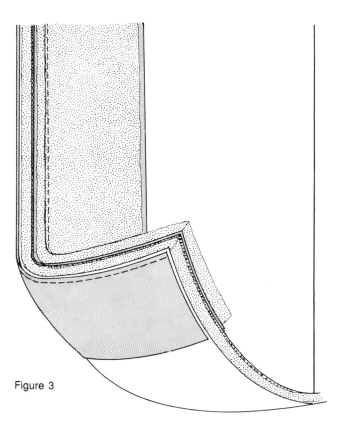

Figure 3

quilt: backing of border, right side up; the quilt, right side up; border top, wrong side up; and, finally, border batting. (Figure 3.) Baste these four layers together and machine stitch. Fold outward the two pieces of border fabric and the batting and baste them together. Do any desired quilting and then finish the raw edges with the edging method of your choice.

Optional Lap Quilting Methods

There are few strict rules in lap quilting, and most of the exceptions fall into the area of assembly. Alternatives to the basic block-to-block, row-to-row assembly described earlier allow you to work with different designs, and they provide a greater challenge to the experienced quilter. Let's explore some novel assemblies and patterns.

PANEL LAP QUILTING

Panel lap quilting is the process of establishing rows to quilt rather than quilting each block individually. Quilting in panels minimizes the handwork on the back of the quilt that must be done in the usual block-to-block step. The long pieces, though, are more cumbersome to handle than the individual blocks and therefore require extra basting.

Machine piece your individual blocks together as usual, and proceed to either add borders (Method A) or sew sets of four blocks together into a larger square (Method B). Working in either horizontal or vertical rows, select the blocks for one row and machine stitch them together, right sides facing, with a ¼" seam allowance.

If you'd like, add a strip of fabric the length of each row to either one or both sides of the row. Cut batting and backing to the size of the row, layer them with the blocks, and baste well. Quilt the row, starting in the center and working towards the ends. Be sure to leave enough unquilted space—½" to 1"—along the outside edges of the row to permit rows to be connected to one another. Once all the rows are quilted, assemble them in the usual row-to-row assembly.

THE DIAGONAL SET

Many quilt patterns take on an entirely new look when the blocks are set in diagonal rows. (Figure 1.) Half-blocks (triangles) form the perimeter of a diagonally assembled quilt. A diagonal setting is not suitable, of course, for blocks with a distinct "up and down" to them, such as Moon Over the Mountain.

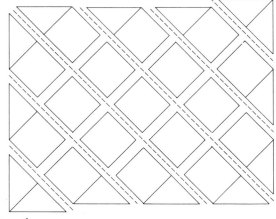

Figure 1

After all of your blocks are pieced, lay them out row by row. Machine stitch the triangular half-blocks to the sides of the blocks they border before lap quilting each block individually. The backing for each of the end blocks—those to which the triangles have been sewn—should be cut so that the diagonal line is on the straight of the grain rather than on the bias.

SQUARE INSETS

A favorite, old-fashioned way of setting a quilt involves the use of square insets between the corners of blocks. While single squares and

The Morning Glory design in an optional setting with nine-patch insets.

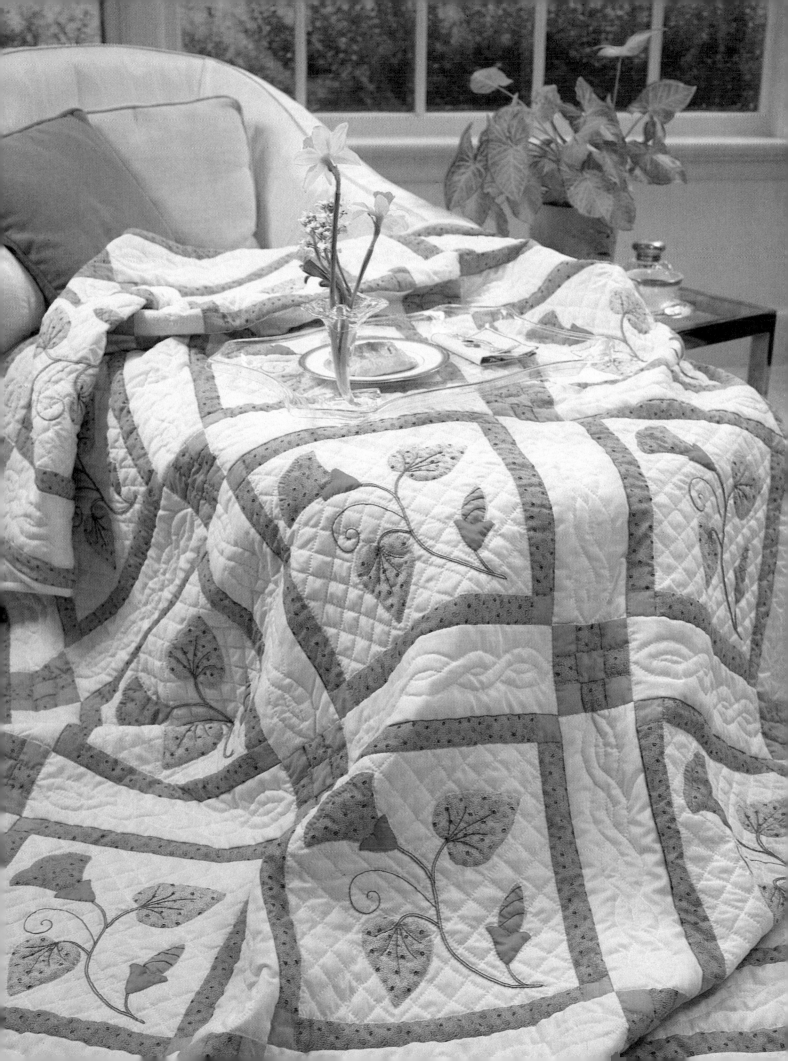

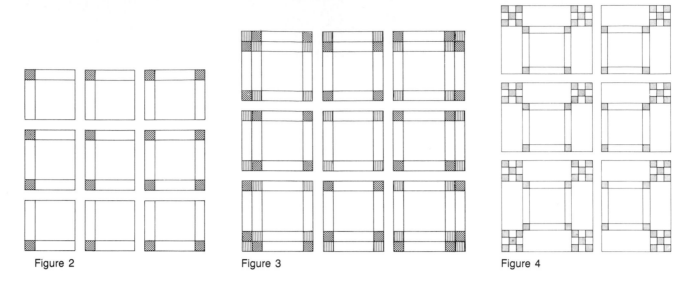

Figure 2   Figure 3   Figure 4

small four-patch insets are most commonly used (Figures 2 and 3), even nine-patch insets are possible (Figure 4).

Because these insets are "shared" by blocks, individual blocks are pieced and quilted with differing numbers of borders. When the blocks are put together, these borders balance with one another to form the total look.

Obviously, it is important to plan ahead. Make a good diagram and follow it to add the appropriate borders to pieced blocks before they are layered with batting and backing. Then use your pieced and bordered blocks as a guide to cutting batting and backing.

The author with the Oh, My Stars quilt on a mountainside near her North Carolina home.

Above left: *Here Comes the Bride wall hanging personalized with an embroidered message.*

Above: *Here Comes the Bride quilt with scalloped edges, a lap quilted adaptation of the traditional Double Wedding Ring design.*

Left: *The Convertible Quilt made as a sampler with inside double-mitered borders.*

The Home, Pieced Home quilt is a study
in variations of a 3" square.

HOME, PIECED HOME QUILT

The Home, Pieced Home Quilt is a study of variations of a 3″ square. The quilt consists of nine rectangular blocks. Each block measures 24½″ x 30½″ and is made up of eight 3″-square patches across and ten 3″ patches down. The finished quilt measures 72″ x 90″.

Start by piecing the picture block in the center of the quilt. With the exception of the sixth and seventh rows across, which must be pieced together as one unit, piece each horizontal row separately. (Consult the photograph on page 98 for suggestions on colors.) When all rows are complete, connect them in the proper arrangement. Appliqué any desired accents, such as the flowers in the lower left.

The Rooster design in each corner (page 29) is appliquéd to the upper section of a 15½″ x 12½″ foundation rather than the usual 12½″-square foundation. Flop your templates when cutting two of the roosters. Appliqué bias tape for the weathervane to the rooster's base and for his crown. Piece together the remainder of each corner block and attach the rooster block. Note that the top left corner block is identical to that on the bottom right except in the way the Rooster faces. Likewise, the top right and bottom left blocks are the same.

Piece together the center blocks on the right and left sides, which are the same. Also piece the identical center blocks on the top and bottom rows.

Layer each pieced block with 24½″ x 30½″ pieces of batting and backing fabric. Baste well and quilt, leaving 1″ on all four sides of the block free of quilting stitches.

Sew blocks together in the usual block-to-block assembly. Finish raw edges with 9 yards of bias edging.

OH, MY STARS QUILT

Oh, My Stars is a lap quilting adaptation of the traditional Lone Star pattern. It is quilted in eight triangular sections, each made up of a pieced diamond and two triangles. (Figure 1.)

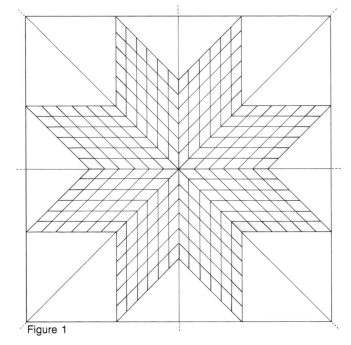

Figure 1

MATERIALS

8 sets of 36 Oh, My Stars diamonds in six different colors. For each set, cut:
    12 Black (Color 1)
    7 Red (Color 2)
    3 Dark Purple (Color 3)
    6 Blue (Color 4)
    5 Yellow (Color 5)
    6 Purple (Color 6)
8 (25⅝″) right-angle triangles in Color 5*
8 (18⅜″) right-angle triangles in Color 5*
8 (43⅛″) right-angle triangles of batting*
8 (43⅛″) right-angle triangles of backing fabric*
*To make a pattern for a right-angle triangle, cut a square from paper or cardboard with its sides measuring the dimension in parentheses. Cut the square in half on the diagonal, forming two right-angle triangles.

METHOD

The finished quilt will be an 84½″ square. If a rectangular quilt is desired, six 14″-square quilt blocks can be attached to two of the ends.

Start by machine piecing together one large star point according to the diagram. (Figure 2.)

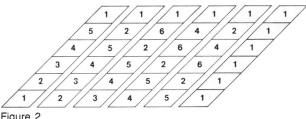

Figure 2

Each point is made up of six rows of six small diamonds. Machine piece each row individually, taking careful note of the order of colors for that row as indicated by the numbers on the diagram. Once all six rows are complete, sew them together in the proper order. (All eight points have the same color and row sequence.)

Once the point is pieced, add the two side triangles. Check the diagram; note that in half of the sections, the large triangle is sewn to the right of the point, while in the other half, it is sewn to the left. (Figure 1.)

Layer the large triangle formed by the pieced point and the two triangles with batting and backing and quilt. After quilting all eight points, assemble the quilt by sewing sets of two points together, forming four squares. Then assemble the squares.

HERE COMES THE BRIDE QUILT

After being asked many times if the popular Double Wedding Ring design could be lap quilted, I decided to devise a way of making it in small, workable sections. Each block is a 20½″ square consisting of forty-eight pieces, so it is not easy to piece. An experienced seamstress may wish to undertake it, or a group of quilters may make it a special project. Twenty members of the Landrum (South Carolina) Quilters Club, for instance, each contributed one block to the quilt pictured on page 97; their finished quilt measures 90″ × 110″.

MATERIALS (For one 20½″ block)
4 Bride Piece As in muslin or other light fabric
4 Bride Piece Bs in same fabric as Piece A
8 Square Gs in yellow or other bright fabric
16 Bride Piece Es, 8 light and 8 dark
16 Bride Piece Ds, 8 light and 8 dark
1 (20½″-square) piece of batting
1 (20½″-square) piece of backing fabric
Note: Eight piece Cs, four light and four dark, can be substituted for the piece Es and Ds.

METHOD

Machine stitch two E and two D pieces together according to the diagram. (Figure 1.)

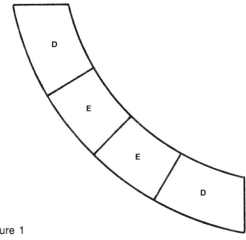

Figure 1

Repeat this process until you have eight segments, four light and four dark, made up of four pieces each. (This step is not necessary if you are substituting C pieces for E and D pieces.)

Sew a G piece to both ends of the four *light* segments. (Figure 2.)

Sew a B piece to each of the four *dark* segments. (Figure 3.)

Sew one dark segment to each side of two of the A pieces. You will have two semicircles. (Figure 4.)

Add a light segment to each side of each of the two semicircles. (Figure 5.) Sew outward, staggering the seams and connecting the ends of the two G pieces in the process.

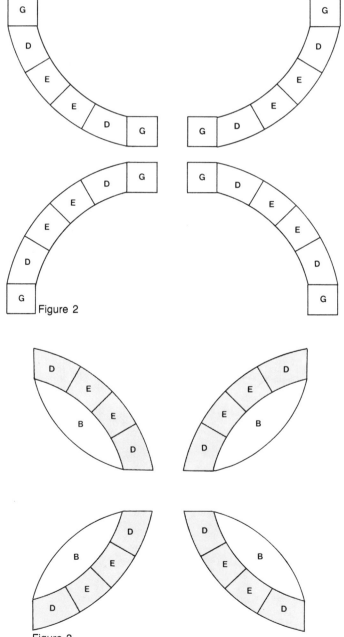

Figure 2

Figure 3

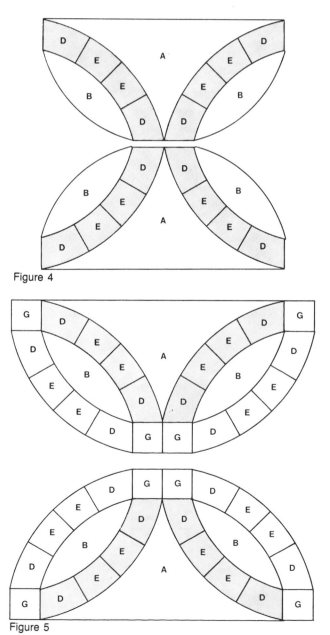

Figure 4

Figure 5

Add both of the remaining A pieces to the outside curve of one of the semicircles. (Figure 6.) Pin the remaining semicircle in place, aligning the seams between the G pieces. Machine stitch this curved connection from the center out.

Layer the pieced block with batting and backing. Baste well and quilt.

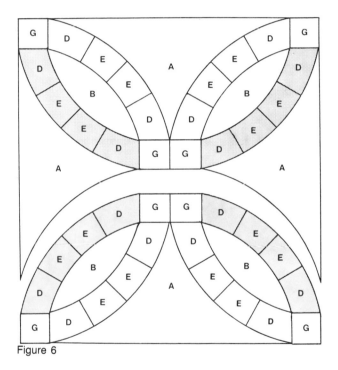

Figure 6

THE CONVERTIBLE QUILT

The Convertible Quilt is a year-round bed cover created without a single quilting stitch. Based on the European custom of using a *duvet*, it is much like a very large pillowcase with a patchwork top. In winter, put a loose filler (*duvet*) inside and it becomes a warm comforter. In warm weather, take the filler out and it is a decorative coverlet.

MATERIALS

12½"-square pieced blocks with mitered borders
Muslin squares cut the size of bordered blocks
Backing fabric the size of quilt top
Snap tape the width of quilt top
Comforter or *duvet* the size of quilt top

METHOD

Piece together the 12"-square blocks of your choice and add a mitered border around all four sides of each block. Measure your bordered block and cut a square of muslin the same size. Lay the bordered block and the muslin wrong sides together. Using the zipper foot on your sewing machine and a coordinating color of thread, attach the block to the muslin by stitching a line very close to the seam between the pieced block and its border. (Figure 1.)

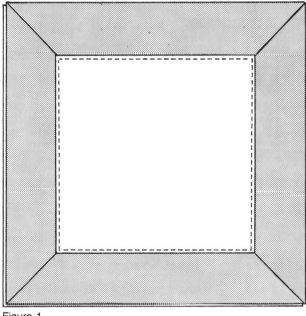

Figure 1

Figure 2

To assemble these two-layered blocks, lay two blocks right sides together. Machine stitch an overedge (overcast) zigzag seam so that raw edges will be finished in the process. (Figure 2.) Connect blocks to form rows, and connect rows with the same overedge seam. If you wish, add a border to the entire perimeter of the assembled spread.

Cut a backing the size of the assembled spread. (You will probably need to seam together two widths of fabric or use a large bed sheet.) Lay the backing and the spread right sides together. First baste and then machine stitch a seam on both sides and one end. On the other end, stitch a small hem on both layers of fabric. Sew snap tape over these two hems so that you will be able to easily open and close your convertible quilt; then turn it right side out.

For winter use, put a *duvet* inside the case. *Duvets* are offered in many home furnishings catalogues. If you are unable to find one, any comforter will do.

If the *duvet* slips around in the case, sew lengths of ribbon on the corners of the *duvet* and another set of ribbons to the inside corners of the case; tie sets together.

Quick Quilted Projects

Small projects using one, two, or three quilt blocks are very appealing for one big reason: They're finished in a flash. The husband of one of my students pointed out to her that if she'd just connect all the pillows she had made, she'd have a finished quilt. Like many of us, though, she loved small projects and the ways she could decorate her home and accessorize her wardrobe with them.

Most of the projects in this chapter were made with the Moon Over the Mountain design, but any of the designs in this book can be used. Don't be afraid to experiment a little—embellish your pieced blocks with appliquéd accents and interesting quilting lines.

TOTE BAGS

MATERIALS
2 (12½"-square) pieced blocks with 3½"-wide mitered borders, quilted to batting and backing
2½ yards of 2½"-wide continuous bias strips for edging
2 (3" x 18") continuous bias strips for handles
2 (3" x 18") pieces of batting
2 (19" or longer) selvage strips or shoelaces

METHOD
Align the two blocks, right sides together, and pin. Fold the 2½"-wide bias strip in half lengthwise. Align its raw edges with the raw edges of three sides of the blocks.

First baste and then machine stitch the two blocks and the bias strip together. Turn the bias strip over the raw edges and slip stitch it into place. (Figure 1.)

Measure 2" from the bottom corner up the side seam and mark with a pin; then measure 2" from the corner across the bottom seam and mark. Align these two seams, matching the pins. Machine stitch a straight line, perpendicular to the seams, at the point where the pins

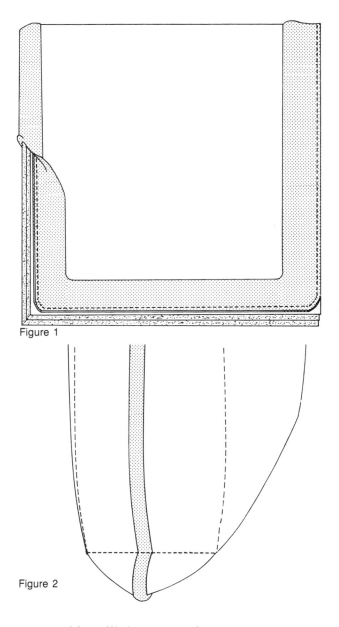

Figure 1

Figure 2

meet; this will leave a triangular extension. (Figure 2.) Now turn the tote bag right side out; your corners will be boxed.

For each handle, fold a 3" x 18" strip of bias lengthwise, right sides together. Place a long strip of selvage or a shoelace inside of the fold and pin it in place. (Be sure the selvage or shoelace is long enough to extend a little from each end.)

Place the piece of batting under the folded bias. Machine stitch the bias and batting together at one end (catching the selvage or shoelace); pivot the needle and stitch down the side. (Figure 3.) Be sure the batting remains on the

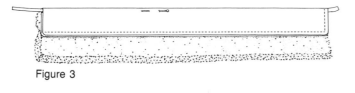

Figure 3

bottom against the feed dogs. A lockknit stitch or tiny zigzag stitch works well.

By slowly pulling the selvage or shoelace that extends from the unsewn end, the handle will invert. It can be left puffy or it can be topstitched by machine for a flatter look. Pin each end of the handle in place on the top of the bag, about 5″ from the side seams.

Complete the top, raw edges of the tote bag with a double fold of 2½″-wide bias fabric applied in the same manner as that on the inside edges.

HANDBAGS

MATERIALS
3 (12½″ square) pieced blocks
1 (2½″ x 12½″) piece of fabric for bottom panel
1 (12½″ x 39½″) piece of batting
1 (12½″ x 39½″) piece of muslin for backing
1 (12½″ x 39½″) piece of fabric for lining
Macrame, chain, or cloth handle

METHOD
Machine stitch the three pieced blocks and the bottom panel end to end into a long rectangle. (Figure 1.) If the blocks you are using have a distinct up and down in their design, such as the Moon Over the Mountain, take that into account. Mark quilting lines if you need them. (For a crazy patch bag, piece together one long

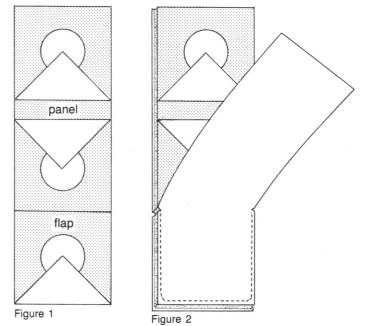

Figure 1

Figure 2

rectangle rather than using three quilt blocks. An attractive evening bag can be made from a 9½″ x 20½″ crazy patch block.)

Baste batting and muslin backing to the long rectangle and quilt. Trim off any excess batting and draw a perfect 12″ x 39″ rectangle on the muslin with a fabric marker to indicate a ¼″ seam allowance. If you would like a rounded or oddly shaped flap, it should be shaped at this point.

Using a fabric marker, make a mark on each side of the muslin indicating where the flap block ends. Place the lining and quilted flap right sides together and baste securely. Machine stitch around the three outside edges of the flap, backstitching at the points where the flap ends. Trim the edges and clip into the fabric ¼″ where the backstitching ends. (Figure 2.)

Turn the flap right side out and hand quilt along the three outside seams. This step prevents the lining from sagging.

Turn the two remaining quilt blocks right sides together, with the fold at the center of the bottom panel you've sewn between them. Fold

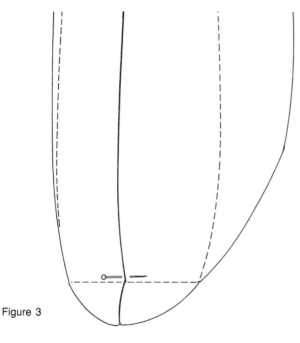

Figure 3

Pieced Little Dutch Boy and Dutch Girl are good candidates for tote bags.

the remaining lining fabric right sides together, with its fold aligned with the fold on the bottom panel. Pin and baste these layers together. Machine stitch the two side seams with a ¼" seam allowance, taking care to sew as close as possible to the flap.

Turn the lining fabric right side out, slipping it around the quilted blocks. From each bottom corner, measure 1½" up the side seam and mark that spot with a pin. At each corner, flatten the side seam against the bottom of the bag so that the seam is in the center of the triangle formed; machine stitch a line perpendicular to the seam at the point marked with your pin. (Figure 3.) This step boxes the corners.

Now turn the bag right side out. Turn the raw edges at the top of the bag towards each other and secure them with a running stitch. A cloth handle can be caught at the sides during this step. If you would like a macrame or chain handle, sew bias loops to the sides through which it can be strung.

A tiny tote bag is made from the quarter section of a four-patch block.

Coffee Cup place mats for the breakfast table.

PLACE MATS

MATERIALS
1 (12½"-square) pieced block
2 (4" x 12½") pieces of fabric for sides
1 (12½" x 19½") piece of fabric for backing
1 (12½" x 19½") piece Pellon® fleece

METHOD
You may want to make several place mats in the same design or make different designs in the same fabrics.

Machine stitch the two side rectangles to either side of the pieced block, right sides together. Press the block, front and back. (If your table is round or oval, a rectangular place mat will hang over the edge; you may wish to cut the right angle from each corner, forming an octagonal place mat.)

Transfer any stencil patterns onto the front of the place mat for a quilting guideline. Consider tracing a knife, fork, and spoon design for quilting.

Pin and baste the Pellon® fleece to the wrong side of the backing fabric. Align the backing and the top of the place mat, right sides together. Machine stitch these layers together on all sides with a ¼" seam allowance, leaving a 4" opening on one side. (Be sure to leave the needle in the fabric when you pivot at the corners.) Trim the edges to an ⅛" seam allowance on all sides.

Turn the place mat right side out through the 4" opening; close the opening with a slip stitch. Hand quilt a line ¼" inside all of the outside edges. Baste the place mat well and quilt from the center outward, following the stencil pattern previously marked.

Quarter sections of the Four Seasons design used in an apron with string quilting accents and in a table runner.

*Moon Over the Mountain and Four Seasons blocks com-
bine beautifully in vests. Add appliqué accents, log cabin
borders, or string quilting for variety.*

Left: *Show off your snapshots in a photo album with a quilted cover.*
Below: *Moon Over the Mountain and Four Seasons blocks take on a variety of looks as pillows, place mats, and patchwork pictures.*

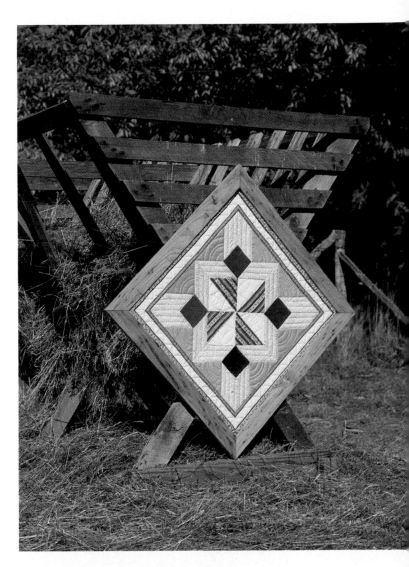

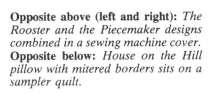

Above: *A flanged pillow has mitered borders quilted to the pillow back.*
Right: *A patchwork picture made with a variation of the Formal Garden design.*
Below: *Dresden Plate pillow and freehand patchwork picture pick up the quilt's monochromatic color scheme.*

Opposite above (left and right): *The Rooster and the Piecemaker designs combined in a sewing machine cover.*
Opposite below: *House on the Hill pillow with mitered borders sits on a sampler quilt.*

*Roman shade in the Moon Over the Mountain design.
String quilted accents and different fabrics in each block
show the changing seasons.*

ROMAN SHADES

MATERIALS

4 (12½"-square) Moon Over the Mountain blocks with string quilting accents (See note below.)

26 (2½" × 12½") strips of fabric for borders

40 (2½"-square) patches of fabric for corner accents

2 (16½" × 20½") pieces of white backing fabric

2 (16½" × 20½") pieces of batting

2 (18½" × 20½") pieces of white backing fabric

2 (18½" × 20½") pieces of batting

2 yards of bias edging

Ring tape

METHOD

Note: Piece each of the four Moon Over the Mountain blocks from different fabrics, using string quilted sections (page 53) that will convey the feeling of the four seasons.

Add the off-balance borders and square insets. (Figure 1.) Note that the top and bottom blocks have more borders than the two middle blocks.

Layer each block with backing and batting fabric and quilt. (The larger pieces of batting and backing will fit the top and bottom blocks, the smaller pieces the two middle blocks.)

Sew the blocks together using the block-to-block assembly technique (page 87) and finish off the raw edges with bias edging. Slip stitch two rows of ring tape to the back of the blocks, being careful not to go through to the front. Your local drapery store can advise you on the hardware needed to hang your finished shade.

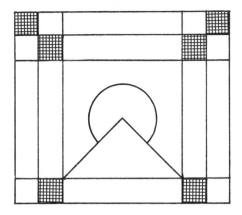

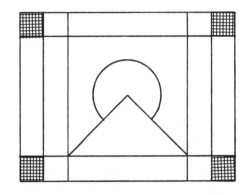

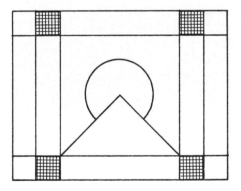

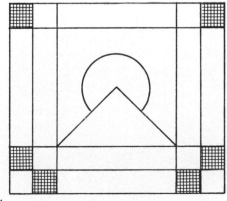

Figure 1

TABLE RUNNERS

You can make a table runner of any length by sewing several pieced blocks end to end in a long rectangle. Add a border if you wish and then cut backing and batting the same size as the rectangle. Baste the three layers together from the center outward and proceed to quilt. Finish raw edges with bias tape or a double-folded bias strip.

APRONS

The bib of a pinafore-style apron is the perfect place to show off a favorite quilt block. Using a standard apron pattern, cut a lining (backing) from the pattern piece for the bib. Place the quarter section of a four patch block in the center of the pattern piece to determine how much border fabric to add in order to fill up the pattern piece. Sew on borders; cut a piece of batting as large as the area you wish to quilt and baste it in place to the wrong side of the bordered block. Then lay the bordered block on the lining, wrong sides together, baste, and quilt. Consider quilting the waistband and string quilting the pockets.

VESTS

A quilted vest is made much like any other lined vest. The trick is in knowing how to piece the outside fabrics together and when to quilt.

Choose a simple, box-style vest pattern that has no darts. Cut all of the pattern pieces except the lining from a foundation material—either Pellon® fleece (for a warm vest) or muslin.

Baste a pieced block directly onto the foundation for the back of the vest. The block can be placed on the straight or on the diagonal, whichever you prefer. The rest of the foundation must now be covered. You may wish to add

a series of borders to the block or you may prefer to cover the exposed portions of the foundation with one fabric. In either case, add fabric in the "sew and flip" manner—lay it right side down on top of your pieced block, machine stitch a seam right through to the foundation, and then flip the added fabric back so its right side is up. When the entire foundation piece is covered, trim any pieces of fabric that extend beyond its bounds and mark the quilting pattern. If you are using Pellon® fleece, trim the fleece about ¼″ all around to permit smoother connection of seams.

Cover the foundations for the two front pieces of the vest in the same manner as you did for the back. Two or even three patches of a four patch pattern can be placed on each side. A pattern that does not have an obvious center division, such as the Moon Over the Mountain, must be pieced in two separate sections, since cutting the block in half would not allow for a ¼″ seam allowance where each half meets the center. You will have to take into account this seam allowance when cutting the pieces for each half, adding ¼″ to each piece that you are cutting in half because it meets the center. (Figure 1.) (In Moon Over the Mountain, those

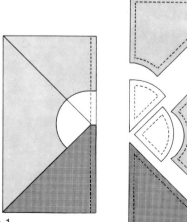

Figure 1

pieces are the center sky and moon pieces and the mountain.)

Follow the assembly directions in your vest pattern to sew together and insert the lining in your vest. Once the lining is in place, invert the vest through seams left open either in the underarm or shoulder area.

Quilt your vest after the vest is inverted and before the remaining seams are connected because it is much easier to work on a flat surface. Baste well and hand quilt around all of the concealed seams at least ¼" from the edge to set the lining in place. Be sure to keep your stitches far enough from the remaining raw edges to permit connection of the remaining seams. Start quilting the interior sections of the vest at the center of the back and work outward.

PHOTO ALBUM COVERS

MATERIALS

2 (12½"-square) pieced blocks
1 (12½" × 25") piece of batting
1 (12½" × 25") piece of fabric for backing
2 (2½" × 7") bias strips for handles
2 (2½" × 7") pieces of batting for handles
2 (25"-long) pieces of narrow grosgrain ribbon
2 (11½" × 12½") pieces of fabric for flaps
2 feet of 2½"-long continuous bias for binding
   edges
1 (11" x 11½" x 2") photo album

METHOD

Machine stitch the two pieced blocks together along one edge. Press and mark them with desired quilting lines.

First baste and then quilt the pieced blocks to the batting and backing fabric. If a ruffle is desired, baste it to the top of the blocks, right sides together.

Prepare handles in the method described for tote bags (see page 105) and pin them to the

fronts of the blocks, positioning each handle end about 3½" in from the side.

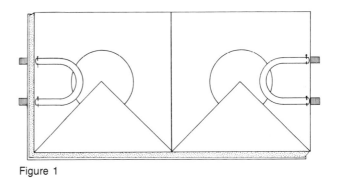

Figure 1

Place ribbons on the back side of the blocks. Pin each end at the point where the handles are anchored at the outside. (Figure 1.) (The ribbons will bear the weight of the album and keep the handles from stretching the fabric.)

Hem one long side of each of the flap sections. Align the remaining raw edges of each of the flaps with the outside edges of the blocks with right sides together. Machine stitch along the three outside edges of each flap to secure the flap, the ribbons and the handles.

Invert the flaps so they are on the wrong side of the blocks. Complete the remaining raw edges of the blocks with the bias strip. Fold it in half lengthwise, align its raw edges with the raw edges of the blocks and machine stitch; turn the strip around the edges and slip stitch into place. Slip the cover of the photo album into the flaps.

PATCHWORK PICTURES

MATERIALS

1 (12½"-square) pieced block
Wood picture frame
Fabric for borders
Batting
Backing fabric
Bias tape
Staple gun

METHOD

Machine piece your block. Try cutting some of the geometric shapes from muslin and string quilting them (page 53).

Measure the inside perimeter of your picture frame. The border for your block should be large enough so that the finished block will be slightly larger (about ½″ all around) than the inside of the frame.

Quilt your bordered pieced block to batting and backing fabric. Bind the raw edges with bias tape.

Staple the block directly to the back of the frame.

SEWING MACHINE COVERS

MATERIALS

1 (12½″-square) Rooster block
1 (12½″-square) The Piecemaker block
4 (3″ × 12½″) pieces of border fabric
2 (12½″ × 17½″) pieces of batting
2 (12½″ × 17½″) pieces of backing fabric
2 (8½″ × 10″) pieces of batting for side panels
2 (8½″ × 10″) pieces of backing fabric for side panels
Long strips of colored fabric
3½ yards of bias edging

METHOD

Add a border strip to each side of the two pieced blocks. Layer them with batting and backing and quilt.

Machine stitch the *tops* of the quilted blocks to each other, right sides together. Finish the raw edge of the seam with bias edging.

On one end of each of the two pieces of side panel backing, clip a small amount of fabric from the corners so that this end will curve. Layer batting on the wrong side of each piece. Using the "sew and flip" technique (page 53), machine stitch strips of colored fabric directly to the batting, stitching through to the backing.

Find the midpoint of the curved end of each side panel and align it with the top connecting seam of the quilted blocks. Pin and baste the quilted blocks to the side panels, right sides together. Machine stitch this connection, leaving a raw edge inside. Finish the raw edge of this seam and the raw edges around the bottom with bias edging.

PILLOWS

A 12½″-square pieced block with 3″-wide mitered borders is quickly turned into a pillow with the addition of a sham pillow back and an 18″-square pillow form. Layer the pieced and bordered block with batting and backing and quilt. Cut two pieces of 18½″ × 12″ fabric for the sham backing and sew a ½″ hem on one long side of each. Lay the right sides of the sham backings on the right side of the quilted block so that the hems face center and overlap one another. Align the raw edges of the sham backings with the raw edges of the quilted block and machine stitch along all four sides with a ¼″ seam allowance. Turn the pillow sham right side out and insert the pillow form.

A flanged pillow with flat borders can be made in much the same manner. Before inserting a 12″-square pillow form, though, turn the pillow sham right side out and quilt the borders of the block to the sham backings.

To create a rectangular pillow, place 6½″-square quarter sections of a four patch block side by side and add a border. Two pieces of fabric with a 12″-long zipper sewn between them work best for the back of a rectangular pillow.

Index

Continued on next page.

DESIGNS

Designers & Contributors

Georgia Bonesteel, Hendersonville, NC
Attic Windows quilt, 61
Convertible Quilt, 97
Crazy patch handbags, 1
Here Comes the Bride wall hanging, 97
Home, Pieced Home quilt, 98
Many Miters quilt, 8
Monochromatic quilt, 113
All Quick Quilted Projects, 105-114
Sampler quilts, vi, 60, 112

Mary Boyce, Asheville, NC
King's X quilt, 59

Inez Byrd, Landrum, SC
Star Flower quilt, i
String quilt on horse, 86

Class of 1981, J. C. Campbell Folk School,
Brasstown, NC
Brasstown Star quilt, 83

Nettie Daniel, Landrum, SC
Sampler quilts on floor and child, 8

Flat Rock, NC Ladies' Aid Society and Georgia
Bonesteel
Oh, My Stars quilt, ii, 96

Foster Memorial Seventh Day Adventist Church
Quilters, Asheville, NC
Grandmother's Fan quilt, 62

Women of the Foster Memorial Seventh Day
Adventist Church, Asheville, NC
Sampler quilt for baby, 81

Helen Gage, Tryon, NC
Pinwheel quilt, 84

Lindsay Healy, Upper Montclair, NJ
Sails in the Sunset quilt, 79

Ann Kanipe, Hendersonville, NC
Churn Dash quilt, 81

Esther Klug, Hendersonville, NC
Formal Garden quilt, 80

The Landrum, SC Quilting Group and Georgia
Bonesteel
Here Comes the Bride quilt, 97

Jean Plumley, Landrum, SC
Sampler quilt on table, 8

Tar Heel Piecemakers, Hendersonville, NC
Churn Dash quilt, 85
Saw Tooth Star quilt, 60

Catherine Trawick, Winston-Salem, NC
25-Patch Star quilt, v

Bea Warren, Chandler, NC
Card Tricks quilt, 7

Pat Whitaker, Asheville, NC
Log Cabin quilt, 83

Alice Wortman, Hendersonville, NC
Lavender Lullaby quilt, 2
Morning Glory quilt, 95
White-on-White sampler quilt, 84

Penelope Wortman, Asheville, NC
Dresden Delight quilt, 82

Senior Editor: Candace N. Conard
Editor: Maura C. Kennedy
Design: Steve Logan
Photography: Mac Jamieson
Photo Stylist: Linda M. Stewart
Art: Steve Logan, Don K. Smith,
  Samuel L. Baldwin, David Morrison
Production: Jerry Higdon

122

DECORATING & CRAFT
IDEAS — The Nation's Leading
Craft Magazine ... and a PLUS
for the creative person.

DECORATING & CRAFT IDEAS is about ...

The craft favorites — from stenciling, miniatures and
woodworking, to tole painting, nature crafts and holiday
decorations.

Fashion needlecrafts — for the home or wardrobe. We cover
crochet, knitting, needlepoint, quilting, cross stitch, and more.

Decorating — and how to make your home more inviting. The
monthly features detail simple, yet effective ideas on making the
most of what you have, plus incorporating completed craft
projects into your decor.

Creative cooking — and how to channel your craft talents into
the kitchen. For special times or everyday, our food editors
show you how meals can have creative eye-appeal as well as
fantastic flavor.

Fashion sewing — and how simple it can be to expand a wardrobe and choose the perfect accessories for that "finished
look." Plus tips to make your sewing easier.

To find out how you can receive DECORATING & CRAFT
IDEAS every month, simply write to: DECORATING &
CRAFT IDEAS, P. O. Box C-30, Birmingham, AL 35283

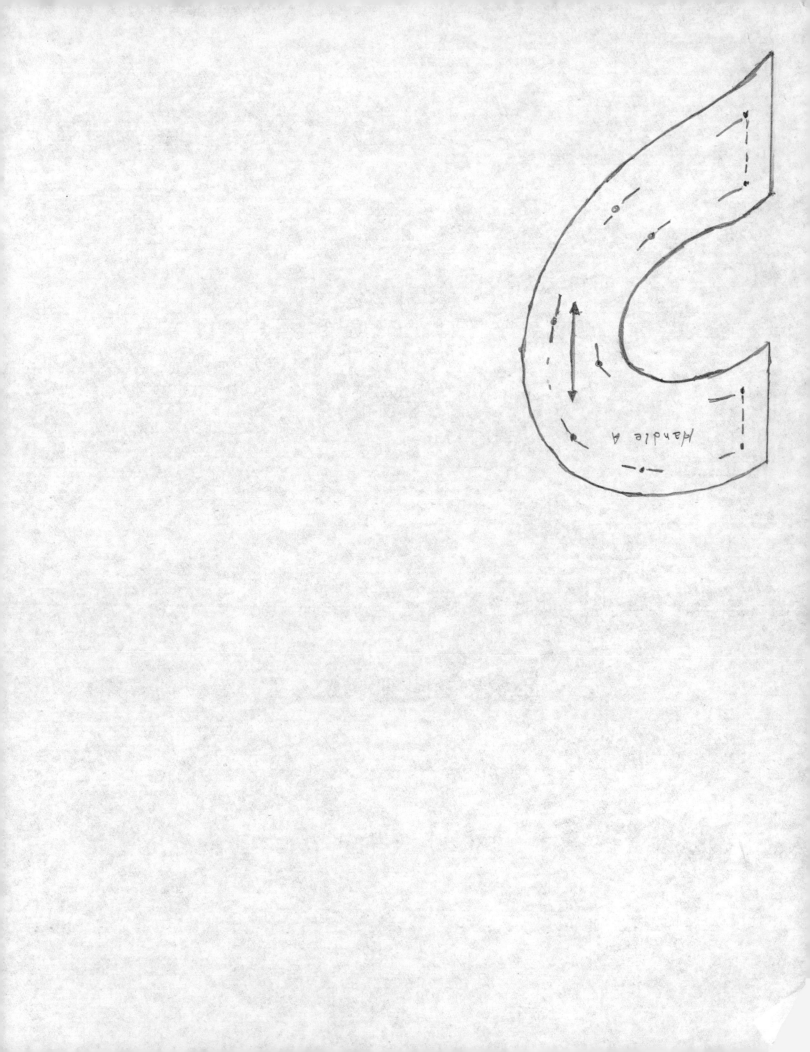

Handle A